Y0-BRR-969

Magic Numbers

Magic Numbers

The 33 Key Ratios That Every Investor Should Know

Peter Temple

John Wiley & Sons (Asia) Pte Ltd

Published in 2002 by John Wiley & Sons (Asia) Pte Ltd
2 Clementi Loop, #02-01, Singapore 129809

Other Wiley Editorial Offices

John Wiley & Sons, Inc., 605 Third Avenue, New York, NY 10158-0012, USA
John Wiley & Sons Ltd, Baffins Lane, Chichester, West Sussex PO19 1UD, England
John Wiley & Sons (Canada) Ltd, 22 Worcester Road, Rexdale, Ontario M9W 1L1, Canada
John Wiley & Sons Australia Ltd, 33 Park Road (PO Box 1226), Milton, Queensland 4064, Australia
Wiley-VCH, Pappelallee 3, 69469 Weinheim, Germany

Library of Congress Cataloging-in-Publication Data
Temple, Peter
Magic numbers: the 33 key ratios that every investor should know / Peter Temple.
p. cm.
Includes index.
ISBN 0-471-47924-1 (cloth: alk. paper)
1. Ratio analysis. 2. Investments–Statistical methods. 3. Investment analysis. I. Title.

HF5681.R25 T45 2001
332.6–dc21 2001026855

Typeset in 12/14 points, Times Roman by Linographic Services Pte Ltd
Printed in Singapore by Craft Print International Ltd
10 9 8 7 6 5 4 3 2

Contents

Acknowledgments

I began my career in finance and the stock market at a time when, in London at least, the science and art of analyzing companies was learnt "on the job". Several colleagues — probably too numerous to mention — have contributed to what understanding I have of the ways in which company accounts should be analyzed.

I should, however, single out for special mention Jeremy Utton of Analyst plc, a UK financial publisher and investment management organization. I contributed to Jeremy's flagship publication for ten years and his insights into company analysis have always been valuable.

The idea for this book came from a conversation I had with Nick Wallwork, my publisher at John Wiley & Sons (Asia). I thank him for setting me on the road to thinking more deeply about how to make financial ratios more accessible to ordinary investors. My editors at Wiley, first Gael Lee and latterly Janis Soo, have proved patient and efficient as the book has progressed to publication. Edward Caruso copyedited the manuscript with great flair.

Acknowledgment should be made to those whose work also forms part of the book: screenshots are by kind permission of Data Dynamics, Calculatorweb, and Winstock Software; the DCF spreadsheet used in "Magic number 30" is adapted from one first devised by Bob Costa.

My wife Lynn contributes her researching talents to all my books. In this instance, thanks are due for her investigation of the web sites where further information on companies and markets can be found. This is mainly contained in the appendix.

A final thank you is also due to Simon London, formerly personal finance editor at *The Financial Times* and now working for the paper in San Francisco. Simon commissioned a 13-week series which contained a number of the ideas in the book and allowed me to try out some of the material on an unsuspecting British readership. Fortunately, the response was favorable.

Needless to say, any errors and omissions that remain are entirely my own doing.

Peter Temple
July 2001

…s" Can

…at used financial jargon … that you knew how to … ought there must be an … ompany by doing a few

…uestions, this book can … argon and, using simple … vs you how to calculate … uing a company's shares

You don't need to be an accountant to understand this book, and any accounting terminology we use will be explained in simple terms. We also highlight any differences in terminology that crop up in the accounts of companies from different countries.

All you need is a basic grasp of how numbers and arithmetic work, an enquiring mind, and the ability to use a calculator.

"Magic Numbers", Companies, and the Stock Market

"Magic numbers", used by stock market analysts and commentators as shorthand for the valuation and financial standing of companies, are often at the intersection of the stock price and the company's official published accounts.

Whether a share is undervalued or overvalued can often be worked out by looking at the share price – an indicator of the value assigned by the stock market to the company – and what the accountants would say is behind its underlying value, its profits and its assets.

Comparing the market's view with the objective numbers the accountants have produced should help you to work out whether a share is cheap or expensive, or if it is somewhere in between.

Equally important, "magic numbers" can be used to compare the value of one company or share with another, providing another insight into whether the shares are cheap, expensive, or valued at about the right level – at least relative to its peers.

The "magic numbers" outlined in this book can all be worked out, using a simple pocket calculator, from share prices available from a daily newspaper and from information provided by companies in their official accounts.

At the end of this book there are some details of how to obtain basic corporate information from print sources and financial web sites. Financial web sites operated by the companies themselves can be a useful source of basic information. Many companies provide an online version of their official accounts.

But don't take the ratios provided by web or print-based statistical services as being entirely reliable. Definitions do vary. We think the ones in this book are the best. And anyway, there is no substitute for calculating the "magic numbers" yourself. It will give you an insight into the way the company functions that is valuable in itself.

Some of the worksheets used in this book are available on the web (a selection is available at *www.magicnumbersbook.com*) for you to download and use, at your own risk, as you see fit. Other useful web addresses are in the appendix at the end of the book.

How This Book is Organized

We have grouped each set of "magic number" sections into a logical sequence. They look in turn at:

- market-based ratios – calculated using the share price together with other relevant accounting information
- profit-based ratios – calculated from the company's profit and loss account or income statement
- balance sheet ratios – calculated using the various components of a company's assets and liabilities
- cash flow-based ratios – calculated from the flows of cash into and out of the business
- other key ratios relating to risk and return commonly referred to in the financial press.

Each of the 33 "magic number" sections contains an overview of the ratios and how they are used.

Each section is organized in the same way. They each contain:

- a definition of the "magic number" in words and symbols
- a definition of its components
- where to find the information needed to calculate it
- a theoretical example of how to calculate it
- an actual example of how to calculate it
- the significance of the "magic number" and how to interpret it.

Will You Use "Magic Numbers" More in Future?

We guarantee it! Recent volatile markets mean that making money is difficult. Researching companies in depth before you buy is the only way to have the comfort that you are picking sound investments.

Investment is also becoming more international. Information on international companies is increasingly being made available on the web. Accountants are getting together to make companies conform to a single global standard. All this means that knowing what the numbers mean can give you an investing edge.

While it may take some time to get complete accounting harmony, even now it is possible to use certain "magic number" techniques to compare companies in different countries. This can help investors to make the right decisions, to assess big companies from their home market, and to compare them with their international peers.

Is NTT cheaper than British Telecom? Is BT cheaper than Deutsche Telecom or BellSouth? Is NTT DoCoMo more expensive than Vodafone? "Magic numbers" can help provide the answers.

A Last Word

Be skeptical! Accounting policies do differ. Even where they don't, companies have considerable latitude as to how they can interpret them. If a "magic number" looks unduly different from one calculated for the same company in the previous year, or for the same ratio at another company, check if there is a reason.

The reason may be an accounting policy change, or just a quirk of the figures. Or it may not be obvious. It could be buried in the small print of the accounts. Detective work may be required.

Anomalies do arise, and often present outstanding investment opportunities. But equally they can signify "creative" accounting that could conceal potential problems. If the accounts seem unduly complex, be suspicious. With experience, you will be able to distinguish between the profitable anomaly and the danger signals.

Part One

Market-Based "Magic Numbers"

MARKET-BASED "MAGIC NUMBERS"

Each of the eight ratios contained in this part looks at the ways in which share prices can be combined with measurements from the various parts of a company's accounts. We can use them to assess whether a stock is cheap or expensive.

The writer Oscar Wilde once defined a cynic as "a man who knows the price of everything and the value of nothing". There is no shortage of cynics in the stock market. But any investor who confuses price with value will probably lose money.

Simply because a share has a low price does not necessarily mean it is a bargain. Similarly, a share with a high nominal price may not be expensive. It is surely easy to grasp that stock prices have to be compared with sales and profit data to have meaning.

"Magic numbers" relating the stock market price of a share to data like this from the company's accounts allow you to distinguish effectively between price and value.

The "magic numbers" outlined in the following pages do precisely this in the following ways:

- Market capitalization and enterprise value (EV) are the basis for many other ratios. Each is an alternative measure of the size of a company, determined by the share price, the number of shares a company has in issue, its cash, and its debt.
- The price-earnings ratio (PER) relates the share price or market value of the company to the annual profits earned (or expected to be earned) by the company.
- Price-earnings growth (PEG) factors relate price-earnings ratios to recent or expected growth in profits earned.
- Dividend yields compare the share price with the dividends paid to shareholders.
- The price to sales ratio (PSR) compares the stock market value of the company with its annual turnover or revenue.

- Enterprise value/Earnings before interest, tax, depreciation, and amortization (EV/EBITDA) compares the "enterprise value" of the business with its operating profits before deducting charges such as interest and tax, or book entries such as depreciation and amortization.
- Price to book value (P/BV) looks at the relationship between the market value of the company and its assets.

These "magic numbers" represent some of the most common ways in which shares are valued. Each has its own importance and each can be given more weight, depending on the type of company being valued.

For those companies with consistent growth, PERs and PEGs may be the best. For slower-growth companies, and for those with a policy of paying out a high proportion of their profits in the form of dividends to shareholders, the dividend yield may be a better measure.

For companies making losses or whose profits are relatively low – perhaps because of high levels of depreciation, amortization, or other book entries – EV/EBITDA is often used as a yardstick.

Remember, however, that none of these measures should be viewed in isolation from the underlying figures from which they are derived, or from other "magic numbers" in this book.

By way of example, take the PSR. Price to sales ratios will be lower for those companies – such as supermarket chains or investment banks – running businesses that have high turnover but make relatively low profits as a percentage of those sales.

Dividend yields will be higher for companies whose financial condition is sufficiently doubtful to suggest that the dividend payments might be reduced in the near future.

Price to book value, or P/BV, is a good yardstick to use for assessing asset-based companies, but care needs to be taken over identifying how the assets in question have been valued.

The sections that follow examine each of the eight "magic numbers" in this part in more depth. Read on to find out how to get the data you need, how to calculate them, and what they mean.

Magic Number

1

Market Capitalization

The Definition

Market capitalization is the stock market value of the company. It is calculated by multiplying the total of issued shares (or common stock) outstanding by their price.

The Formula

Market capitalization = Issued shares outstanding × Share price

The Components

Issued shares (common stock) outstanding – shares that have been issued and can be publicly traded. This includes shares that are "tightly held" by directors and their families, even though these may rarely change hands.

Sometimes market capitalization calculations use what are called "fully diluted" issued shares outstanding. This means that any additional shares that may be issued in the future – for example, as a result of the exercise of executive share options – are also included in the calculation.

Normally you use shares outstanding at the point in time the calculation is performed. You can get these from the annual report. The number should be fully adjusted for any subsequent issues of shares since the company's previous financial year-end. For example, you should take account of any stock splits, or dividends paid in the form of stock instead of cash.

Share (stock) price – the current market price of the shares. This is normally the mid-market price at the close of business on the previous trading day.

Where's the Data?

Issued shares (common stocks) outstanding – these are usually in the notes to the accounts. The note can be found from a reference in the consolidated balance sheet. It will be next to the heading for "called-up share capital" or a similar term. The number of ordinary shares at the end of the year should be taken, and not their nominal money value (if stated).

If the specific number of shares is not stated, you can calculate this by comparing the monetary value with the par value of the shares. For example, monetary value of £10 million for shares with a par value of 10p means that 100 million shares are represented (100 million shares of 10p par value have a nominal money value of £10 million).

The number of shares used to calculate earnings per share should not be used. This will normally be an average for the year, not the most recent figure.

Share (stock) price – from any daily newspaper or financial web site. Take care to use the actual share price and not the prices of any options, warrants, partly paid shares, or other derivatives. Take note also of the units in which the share price is expressed. In the UK shares are traditionally quoted in pence, so a market capitalization expressed in pounds must be adjusted to take account of this.

Calculating It – the Theory

Figure 1.1 shows the different numbers to be pulled from the accounts and how to use them to calculate the ratios.

Figure 1.1 Calculating the "Magic Number" for ... Market Capitalization

Universal Widgets has:

Shares outstanding of	50m
A share price of	£2.50
Market capitalization is	**£125m**
(working)	(50 × 2.5)

CALCULATING IT FOR YAHOO!

Figure 1.2 shows how the highlighted numbers from the accounts of Yahoo! combine to produce the ratios. The company has more information available at its web site (*www.yahoo.com*). Yahoo! is an American global Internet-based communications, commerce, and media company.

Figure 1.2 Calculating market capitalization from Yahoo!'s 1999 Accounts

The figures ... **(in thousands)**	**Dec-31 1999**	**Dec-31 1998**
Assets (p. 33 in the published accounts of Yahoo!)		
Current assets		
Cash and cash equivalents	**233,951**	230,961
Short-term investments	**638,508**	314,822
Stockholders' equity		
Preferred stock, $0.001 par value; 10,000 authorized, none issued or outstanding	**0**	0
Common stock, $0.001 par value; 900,000 authorized, **532,798** and 497,988 issued and outstanding respectively	**533**	498
Yahoo!'s share price at time of writing	**$57**	
The calculation ...		
Market capitalization		**$30,369m**
(working)		(532,798,000 × 57)
Yahoo!'s 532,798 million shares are multiplied by the share price of $57		

The numbers for common stock are confusingly presented. The number of shares is 532,798,000, not 532,798, because the figures in Figure 1.2 are stated to be in thousands. Multiplying the lower figure by the share price of $57 would produce a market capitalization of only $30 million. Common sense tells you this is too low for a company of Yahoo!'s prominence.

What it Means

Market capitalization is a barometer of the company's overall value. More importantly, the position of the company when ranked by market capitalization will determine the stock market index in which it is included and what weight it carries in that benchmark.

Most major stock market indices are capitalization-weighted: the bigger the company, the more influence it has on the index. Companies are keen to see their market value as high as possible. If they are sufficiently large to feature in the market's benchmark index of leading companies, this normally confers extra status and prestige. More practically it means their shares will feature in index-tracking products (usually, for example, mutual funds constructed to mimic a particular index). If so, they will be more highly sought after by influential large investors.

Market capitalization is also the means by which the overall value of the company can be compared directly with the profit and sales figures contained elsewhere in the company's accounts, without the need to reduce those numbers to per-share values. See the section on "price to sales ratio" ("Magic number" 6).

Magic Number

2

Enterprise Value

The Definition

Enterprise value (often abbreviated to EV) adjusts the market capitalization – as described in the previous section – for the balance of any cash or debt the company has. If a company has more debt than cash, the market capitalization increases by the difference between the two numbers. If cash exceeds debt, enterprise value is reduced by that amount.

The Formula

EV = Market capitalization + Total debt − Total cash

The Components

Issued shares (common stock) outstanding – shares that have been issued and are publicly traded. See the expanded definition in the previous section.

Share (stock) price – the current market price of the shares, normally the mid-market price at close of business on the previous trading day.

Total debt – the total of long- and short-term debt issued or owed by the company and its subsidiaries. This could include bank loans and overdrafts, medium- and long-term loans (secured or unsecured), bonds, and all other debts of a similar type.

Cash – cash held in the company's bank account or any liquid investments that can be turned into cash instantly. These would normally include, for example, certificates of deposit (CDs) and other liquid assets, but not investments in shares or other securities whose value could fluctuate sharply from day to day.

Where's the Data?

Issued shares (common stock) outstanding – in the notes to the accounts. The reference to the note in the consolidated balance sheet should be next to the heading "called-up share capital" or a similar term. See expanded definition in the previous section.

Share (stock) price – from any daily newspaper or financial web site. Take care to use the actual share price and not that of any options, warrants, partly paid shares, or other derivatives.

Total debt – from the consolidated (or "group") balance sheet within the heading "accounts receivable", "creditors", or "current liabilities" (for short-term debt), and further down the page for medium- and long-term loans. You may need to look at the relevant note to the accounts. The total debt figure may be the sum of two or three relevant items that must be separately identified.

Cash – from the consolidated (or "group") balance sheet, within the heading "current assets".

Calculating it – the Theory

Figure 2.1 shows the different numbers to be pulled from the accounts and how to use them to calculate the ratio.

Figure 2.1 Calculating the "Magic Number" for ... Enterprise Value

Universal Widgets has:

Market capitalization of	£125m
Short-term debt of	£25m
Long-term debt of	£25m
Cash of	£10m
Enterprise value is	**£165m**
(working)	(125 + 25 + 25 − 10)

CALCULATING IT FOR

NTT

Figure 2.2 shows how the highlighted numbers from this extract from the accounts of NTT combine to produce the "magic number". NTT (*www.ntt.co.jp*) is the largest telephone company in Japan.

Figure 2.2 Calculating Enterprise Value from NTT's 2000 Accounts

The figures ... **(in million ¥)**	**Mar-31** **1999**	**2000**
Assets (p. 38 in the published accounts of NTT)		
Current assets		
Cash and cash equivalents	1,656,672	**1,155,274**
Current liabilities		
Short-term borrowing	235,180	**410,305**
Current portion of LT debt	848,562	**868,648**
Long-term liabilities		
Long-term debt	4,558,358	**4,239,088**
Shareholders' equity (p. 39)		
Common stock, ¥50,000 par value;		
Authorized 62,400,000 shares		
Issued and oustanding		
15,912,000 shares in 1999	795,600	795,600
15,834,590 shares in 2000		
NTT's share price at time of writing		**¥900,000**

The calculations ...

Market capitalization — **¥14,252 bn**
(working) (15.835m × 900,000)

NTT's 15,835 million shares are multiplied by the share price of ¥900,000

Enterprise value — **¥18,615 bn**
(working) (14,252 + 4,239 + 869 + 410 − 1,155 with thousands omitted)

This is NTT's market capitalization of ¥14,252 billion plus short-term borrowings, current portion of long-term debt, plus long-term borrowings minus cash

In the case of NTT the figures appear on the face of the balance sheet. There is no need to refer to the notes to the accounts. The problem with the numbers is working with the heavyweight share price. It means that particular attention must be paid to making sure that like is compared with like when doing the market capitalization calculation and identifying balance sheet numbers.

This is easier to do if thousands are omitted from the calculation and the figures rounded accordingly. If you do this, the workings are reduced to manageable units of a billion yen each. You can then do the calculation with four- and five-figure numbers. A quick check that the calculation is correct is to compare the resulting EV with revenue. Taken from the income statement, this is ¥10,383 billion.

This appears to confirm that the EV calculation is correct. For large telecom companies, the numbers should be broadly the same order of magnitude, as is the case here.

What it Means

Enterprise value has a similar function to market capitalization. The difference is that where market capitalization is based solely around the company's stockholders, equity, enterprise value also includes the bank deposits and amounts contributed by lenders.

You therefore use enterprise value to compare companies on measures that exclude interest paid or received. This is because if interest paid on borrowings (or earned on cash) is not counted in the profit figure, the capitalization of the company must be adjusted to include the impact of the debt (or cash) on the overall total.

The true value of this "magic number" is that it allows you to compare companies in underlying terms, disregarding the impact of their capital structure (the amount of debt or cash in a company's balance sheet). Companies with radically different capital structures can be compared, without the means by which they are financed getting in the way.

These are key building blocks in any financial valuation, and we will return to use them again later in this book.

Magic Number

3

Price–earnings Ratio

The Definition

The *price-earnings ratio* (normally shortened to P/E or PER) is the most common way of valuing a stock. You calculate it by dividing the price of the shares (or stock) by earnings per share. *Earnings per share* (EPS) are the net profits attributable to ordinary stockholders, divided by the number of shares issued.

The Formulas

PER = Share (or stock) price/Earnings per share

EPS = Net income/Issued shares outstanding

The Components

Share (stock) price – the current market price of the shares, normally the mid-market price at close of business on the previous trading day.

Net income – profit attributable to shareholders after deducting tax and minority interests. Minority interests are the profits "owned" by other shareholders in subsidiaries that are less than 100% owned.

Issued shares (common stock) outstanding – shares that have been issued and are publicly traded. This includes shares that are "tightly held" by directors and their families, even though these may rarely change hands.

Sometimes earnings calculations are based on "fully diluted" issued shares outstanding. This takes in, for example, any extra shares that may be issued in the future as a result of the exercise of executive share options and other effects.

Earnings per share calculations normally use "weighted average" shares in issue. This is the average number of shares in issue during the period when the profit was being earned, giving due weight to new shares issued during the period, in accordance with the time they were issued. New shares issued at the beginning of the year carry more weight than those issued at the end. See "Magic number" 11 for more detail on this concept.

WHERE'S THE DATA?

Share (stock) price – from any daily newspaper or financial web site. Take care to use the actual share price and not that of any options, warrants, partly-paid shares, or other derivatives.

Net income – this is found in the profit and loss account (income statement), normally at the bottom of the page. Profit earned for ordinary shareholders (stockholders) should be used. This is the profit figure before any ordinary dividend payments are deducted.

Earnings per share – this is normally stated separately, immediately below the net income figure. If there is a dilution arising from the likely future issue of new shares – for example, as a result of the exercising of executive share options – the earnings per share allowing for this factor may also be separately stated.

Issued shares (common stock) outstanding – you can normally find detailed earnings per share calculations in a note to the accounts referred to from the income statement. The note will often state the weighted average shares issued used in the calculation.

CALCULATING IT – THE THEORY

Figure 3.1 shows the different numbers to be pulled from the accounts and how to use them to calculate the ratio.

Figure 3.1 Calculating the "Magic Number" for ... Price-Earnings Ratio

Universal Widgets has:

Net income of	$100m
Weighted average shares in issue are	20m
Earnings per share are	$5 per share
(working)	(100/20)
Share price is	$80
Price-earnings ratio (PER) is	**16 times**
(working)	(80/5)

CALCULATING IT FOR
DAIMLERCHRYSLER

Figure 3.2 shows how the highlighted numbers from the accounts of DaimlerChrysler combined to produce the "magic number". The company's web site – *www.daimlerchrysler.com* – has more information. DaimlerChrysler is a German/American car manufacturer.

Figure 3.2 Calculating PERs from DaimlerChrysler's 1999 Accounts

The figures ... (in millions, except per share amounts)	**Consolidated (in Euro) Year ended 31 December 1999**	**1998**
Income before extraordinary items (p. 72 in the published accounts of DaimlerChrysler)	**5,106**	4,949
Extraordinary items		
Gain on business disposal, net of tax	659	0
Losses on early repayment of debt	−19	−129
Net income	**5,746**	4,820
Basic earnings per share		
Income before extraordinary items	**5.09**	5.16
Extraordinary items	0.64	−0.13
Net income	5.73	5.03
Diluted earnings per share		
Income before extraordinary items	5.06	5.04
Extraordinary items	0.63	−0.13
Net income	**5.69**	4.91
Note 31 (p. 108)		
Weighted average no. of shares outstanding – basic	**1,002.9**	959.3
Dilutive effect of convertible bonds and notes	10.7	19.8
Shares issued on exercise of options	0	18.3
Shares purchased with proceeds of options	0	−11.8
Shares applicable to convertible preferred stock	0	0.2
Shares contingently issuable	0	1.3
Weighted average no. of shares outstanding – diluted	1,013.6	987.1
DaimlerChrysler's share price at time of writing		**€50.5**

The calculations ...

Price-earnings ratio (basic before extraordinary items)	**9.92**
(working)	(50.5/5.09)

The DaimlerChrysler share price divided by "basic" income before extraordinary items

Price-earnings ratio (fully diluted after extraordinary items)	**8.88**
(working)	(50.5/5.69)

The DaimlerChrysler share price is divided by diluted net income per share

This demonstrates what an elusive concept earnings per share, and hence the price-earnings ratio, can be. The share price remains the same, but the PER calculation varies according to which definition of earnings per share is used.

Extraordinary items are supposed, by definition, to be abnormal. If so, it is legitimate to exclude them from an earnings calculation. But beware that company managers do occasionally include charges that are not extraordinary, but that might otherwise reduce earnings per share.

The real test is whether an item like this is likely to recur year after year. If it is, then it should not be treated as extraordinary.

It is normal to take net income per share before extraordinary items as the bottom half of the fraction. Diluted earnings per share are sometimes used if they make a big difference.

What it Means

The PER is a key ratio for analysts and investors alike. One way of looking at it is that it represents the number of years of profits at the current rate before the price of the shares is recouped in profits earned. This idea is rather notional since these profits will not be returned in full to shareholders.

Another explanation of the PER is simply that it represents the ratio of the market value of the company (see "Magic number" 1) to its after-tax profits.

The PER does enable companies to be compared irrespective of their size, the concept reducing each one to a common currency. This is important because it will, for example, enable the stock market rating of an individual company to be compared with its competitors, and with the market. Stock market index compilers calculate the PER of the index as a whole and of sector groups, so that investors can see how the company's value compares with the market as a whole.

Prospective (that is, forecast) earnings are often used to calculate the PER. The market places a lot of store by these predictions. One reason why stock market analysts are paid huge amounts is because of their supposed skill in forecasting profits. The higher the predicted growth in profit growth, other things being equal, the higher the PER.

If forecast profits turn out to be less than expected, however, the whole basis for the high PER collapses and a sharp downward adjustment takes place. Not only are the profits, and therefore the earnings per share, less than expected, but also growth is less and the justification for the high PER evaporates. The share price is hit hard by this "double whammy".

Dividend Yield

The Definition

The *dividend yield* (usually shortened to "yield") is an alternative way of assessing the value of a share. It is the percentage that the annual dividend paid to shareholders represents of the share price. Dividend yields are always calculated gross (that is, adding back any income tax withheld).

The Formulas

Dividend yield in % = Gross dividend per share × 100/Share (or stock) price

Gross dividend per share = Net dividend per share × "Grossing-up" factor

The Components

Dividend per share – the total of the dividend payments declared for the financial year. This may be one, two, or more separate payments. US companies normally declare dividends quarterly. In the UK and elsewhere, the payment is often in the form of an interim and (usually somewhat larger) final payment. Dividends are normally announced in per-share amounts.

Dividends (or, in the US, dividend rates) are declared at the same time as financial results are announced. The final dividend of one financial year will not therefore be known until the results for that year are announced, early in the following financial year.

It is normal to use the dividends for the last complete financial year as the basis for the dividend calculation. In the case of US companies, the norm is to use four times the latest announced quarterly rate.

Share (stock) price – the current market price of the shares, normally the mid-market price at close of business on the previous trading day.

Grossing-up factor – this figure is calculated by using the rate of tax deducted from dividends *before the investor receives them.* The dividend declared (and stated in the company accounts) is the "net" dividend (that is, after deduction of tax). To arrive at the gross dividend, the net dividend is multiplied by a "grossing-up" factor. You calculate this using the formula:

Grossing-up factor = 100/(100 − percentage tax rate deducted)

If, as in the UK, dividends are paid net of a 20% tax deduction, the grossing-up factor is 100/(100 − 20); that is, 100/80, or 1.25. A net dividend of 10p per share is equivalent to a gross dividend of 12.5p per share. The "grossed-up" figure is the one used to calculate the dividend yield.

Where's the Data?

Net dividend – in some company accounts the *per-share* dividend is stated in the income statement. If it isn't, it can usually be found in a note to the accounts. The number of the relevant note should be given in the income statement alongside the entry for the cash cost of the dividend.

Often, however, the per-share dividend total for the year will be included in a "financial highlights" table at the front or back of the document. In the note to the accounts, how the dividend splits between interim and final, or by quarterly payment, should be spelt out in detail.

Share (stock) price – from any daily newspaper or financial web site.

Grossing-up factor – a stockbroker should be able to advise on the tax treatment of dividends. An easy method of working this out for yourself is to calculate the yield on the dividend as stated in the accounts and compare it with the yield calculation as stated in the financial pages of a newspaper. Use the same share price for both calculations. Any difference should reflect the difference between the gross and net figures. Compare two different companies in this way as a check.

Calculating it – the Theory

Figures 4.1a and 4.1b show the different numbers to be pulled from the accounts and how to use them to calculate the ratio.

Figure 4.1a Calculating the "Magic Number" for ... Dividend Yield (using grossing up)

Universal Widgets has:

Net dividend of 10p
Tax rate on dividends of 20%
A share price of 250p
Gross dividend yield is 5%
(working) .... ((10 × 1.25* × 100)/250)
* 1.25 is the grossing-up factor of 100/100 – 20

Figure 4.1b Calculating the "Magic Number" for ... Dividend Yield (quarterly dividend)

Universal Widgets has:

Quarterly dividend rate of $2.50
Tax rate on dividends of 0%
A stock price of $200
Dividend yield is 5%
(working) .... ((2.50 × 4*) × 100/200)
* quarters

CALCULATING IT FOR GREAT UNIVERSAL STORES

Figure 4.2 shows how the highlighted numbers from this extract from the accounts of Great Universal Stores (GUS) combine to produce the "magic number". GUS (the web address is *www.gusplc.co.uk*) is a UK-based retail and business information company.

Figure 4.2 Calculating Dividend Yield from Great Universal Stores' 2000 Accounts

The figures ...

Note 10. **Dividends** (p. 51 in the published accounts of GUS)	**2000 £m**	**1999 £m**
Interim paid – 6.2p per share (1999 6.2p)	62.4	62.4
Final proposed – 14.4p per share (1999 14.4p)	144.8	144.8
Total – 20.6p per share (1999 20.6p)	207.2	207.2
Great Universal Stores' share price at the time of writing		**520p**

The calculation ...

Gross dividend yield **4.95%**
(working) (20.6 × (100/100 – 20) × 100/520)

GUS's total dividend of 20.6 is multiplied by the grossing-up factor of 100/80, multiplied by 100, and then divided by the share price of 520p

How you calculate the dividend yield does differ from market to market. In the US, the norm is to calculate the dividend based not on what was paid in the past but on the assumption that the current quarterly dividend rate will continue.

You can find yields in the financial columns of daily newspapers and calculations can be checked easily. Even so, you need to understand how these figures are arrived at.

Remember that grossing-up factors (where they apply) are a constant. They only change when tax rates change.

What it Means

Similar comments apply to dividend yields as to the price-earnings ratio. Like PERs, yields enable companies to be compared irrespective of their size, reducing each one to a common basis.

This is important because it will, for example, enable the dividend-based stock market rating of an individual company to be compared with those of its competitors, with that of the market, and indeed with bond yields. Stock market index compilers calculate the yields of the index as a whole, and of sector groups. Hence, you can see how a company's yield compares to that of the market.

Yield is important too, because it is the actual cash return you receive from a company. It can be directly compared with other investments that offer cash returns, such as government bonds or savings accounts. Yields on shares are usually lower than the yields on government bonds. This is mainly because, while the income from bonds is fixed, dividend payments can grow as a company's profits rise.

Dividends can also be reduced, however, and a very high yield may indicate a danger of the dividend being cut. Equally, yields of companies that are growing slowly will tend to be higher, and more comparable with bond returns, because the scope for dividend growth is more limited. High-growth companies, if they pay dividends at all, will tend to have low yields for the opposite reason.

Investors sometimes look at what is termed "total return". The total return is the dividend yield derived from the shares based on the past year's dividend plus the share price appreciation (or lack of it) seen in the shares over the same period.

Looking ahead, total return can be estimated by assuming that the shares will stand on the same multiple of earnings in 12 months' time, as they do now. Total return is then the expected percentage earnings growth over the period plus the expected dividend yield. However, a calculation like this is tenuous and should be treated warily.

PEG Factor

The Definition

The PEG ratio, sometimes called the *PEG factor*, relates the price-earnings ratio (PER) to the growth rate of the company. It is normally calculated on a "prospective" or forecast basis. This means you divide the PER based on forecast earnings by expected percentage growth in earnings per share. For instance, if the prospective PER were 15 times and the forecast earnings growth was 20%, the PEG factor would be 0.75.

The Formulas

PEG factor = price-earnings ratio (times)/Earnings Growth (in %)

Forecast PEG = price-earnings ratio (on forecast earnings)/Earnings growth (% change from last reported year to current year)

The Components

Price-earnings ratio – see the calculation performed in "Magic number" 2. The price-earnings ratio (or PER) is the current share price divided by earnings per share. "Historic" PERs are the current share price divided by the latest reported earnings per share. "Prospective" PERs are the current share price divided by forecast earnings for the current financial year.

Earnings growth – this is *either* a long-term average of earnings growth in prior years, *or* the growth in the last reported financial year compared to the previous one, *or* the growth in earnings expected in the current (as yet incomplete) financial year compared with the last reported full year.

The PEG calculation must pair up the appropriate PER with the comparable growth rate: historic PER with historic growth, or prospective PER with prospective growth.

Where's the Data?

Share (stock) price – from any daily newspaper or financial web site. Care should be taken to use the actual share price.

Earnings per share (last reported year or historic record) – normally found in the income statement towards the bottom of the page. The historic record of earnings per share figures may be contained in a table of financial highlights at the beginning or end of the accounts. Growth rates are the percentage changes from one year to another or, for a span that covers more than two years, the average compound annual growth rate for the period in question.

Earnings per share (forecast) – a consensus of market estimates should be used. This can be found, especially for major companies, in commonly used statistical services or at financial web sites such as Yahoo! Finance. See the appendix for the web addresses of some commonly used statistical services of this type.

CALCULATING IT – THE THEORY

Figure 5.1 shows the different numbers to be pulled from the accounts and how to use them to calculate the ratio.

Figure 5.1 Calculating the "Magic Number" for ... the PEG Factor

Tokyo Widgets has:

Financial years ending December	**Reported 1999**	**Reported 2000**	**Forecast 2001**
Earnings per share for these years are	¥22	¥25	¥35
Earnings per share growth is therefore		14%	40%
(working)		((25 × 100/22) – 100)	((35 × 100/25) – 100)
The share price is		¥600	
Price-earnings ratio (PER) is		24.0	17.1
(working)		(600/25)	(600/35)
PEG factor (based on historic PER and growth) is		**1.7**	
(working)		(24/14)	
PEG factor (based on forecast PER and growth) is			**0.43**
(working)			(17.1/40)

CALCULATING IT FOR
AJINOMOTO

Figure 5.2 shows how the highlighted numbers from this extract from the accounts of Ajinomoto combine to produce the "magic number". There is more information at *www.ajinomoto.com*. Ajinomoto is a Japanese company manufacturing food and amino acid products.

Figure 5.2 Calculating the PEG Factor from Ajinomoto's 2000 Accounts

The figures ...

Six-year summary of selected financial data (p. 24 in the published accounts of Ajinomoto)	**2000**	**1999**	**1998**
Per share (yen)			
Net income	**27.2**	**20.4**	27.7
Shareholders' equity	624.6	608.9	603.0
Cash dividends	10.0	12.0	10.0
Ajinomoto's share price at the time of writing		**¥1,223**	

The calculation ...

PEG factor (based on historic earnings and growth)		**1.35**	
(working)	(1,223/27.2)/((100 × 27.2/20.4) − 100)		

Ajinomoto's historic PER of 45 times (1,223/27.2) is divided by earnings growth of 33.3% from 20.4 to 27.2

If the company's earnings growth was the same in 2001 as in 2000, earnings per share would be ¥36.3, the PER would fall to 33.7 times, and the PEG, on the same 33% earnings growth rate, would drop to 1.01

The major problem with PEGs relates to the passage of time.

A prospective PEG taken at the beginning of the financial year contains earnings figures that will not be proved right or wrong for perhaps another 12 months.

This clearly has a different validity to a PEG taken near the end of the financial year. In this case, the results for that year will be announced in a matter of weeks. Usually, by this time the consensus forecast has already been adjusted to reflect information that has emerged in the course of the year.

Comparing the PEGs on companies with different year-ends is particularly difficult because of this factor.

One solution is to use a PEG calculated only on already-reported earnings growth.

There are two alternatives. Either use an up-to-the-minute calculation of earnings and earnings growth adding up the last two half years or last four reported quarters to make the figures as current as possible. Or use a long-term average of earnings growth over, say, the previous five years. Either way, this calculation does get complicated.

However, there is a big objection to using historic figures. PEGs are really used for working out the right price to pay for *expected* growth.

Jim Slater, the British investment guru who invented the idea of the PEG, suggested the best way to solve this problem: take the average earnings expected for the two following forecast years, weighting the calculation either one way or the other, depending on when in the year it is done, and then work out earnings growth and PER and PEG based on these figures.

There is no simple way around this problem, although Slater's book, *Investment Made Easy*, explains his concept in more detail.

What it Means

PEGs are a guide as to whether or not what you are paying for growth is reasonable. Slater's original yardstick was that the PER should be less than the earnings growth number. In other words, with a PEG of less than one, a stock starts to look cheap. The lower the number, the cheaper it gets.

This has an elegant simplicity that cannot be faulted, even though one might argue about how to deal with time differences. Interpreting PEGs, like many other "magic numbers", is often "refined" to justify excessive market valuations. Our view is that this is mistaken. If profit growth is absent, or slow, then a low multiple of the profit is all that can be justified.

PEGs only work with certain types of company. If a company is currently making losses, or if its profits are falling, or if it is habitually valued on the basis of its assets or by some other measure, then the PEG will be of little or no use. It works best when comparing growth companies.

Price to Sales Ratio

The Definition

The *price to sales ratio* (PSR), sometimes known as the "revenue multiple", is the market capitalization of the shares divided by the company's annual sales. An alternative definition is share price divided by sales per share. Other common terms for sales are "turnover" and "revenue".

The Formulas

PSR = Market capitalization/Annual sales

or

PSR = Share price/Sales per share

The Components

Market capitalization – this is the stock market value of the company. It is calculated by multiplying the total of issued shares (or common stock) outstanding by their price (see "Magic number" 1). To recap, the components of this calculation are: *issued shares (common stock) outstanding* – shares that have been issued and are capable of being publicly *traded*; and the *share (stock) price* – the current market price of the shares, normally the mid-market price at the close of business on the previous trading day.

Annual sales – sales, revenue, or turnover are virtually interchangeable terms and are in such common use as to need little further explanation. Where calculations differ is in whether or not, in performing this calculation, you take the sales for the last reported year, or the last 12 months.

Using the last 12 months' figures is common practice for US companies because they report quarterly. In this case, the figure to take (assuming a forecast is not used) would be the cumulative sales for the preceding four reported quarters. In other words, if a company has recently announced third-quarter sales, the last 12 months' sales figures would be the sales for the nine months of the current year plus the fourth quarter of the previous one. For companies reporting twice yearly, if a half-year has been reported, sales in the first half of the current year would be added to those of the second half of the previous one.

Where's the Data?

Annual sales – normally the top-most figure or subtotal in the consolidated profit and loss account or income statement. Any sales deriving from large one-off business disposals may distort the figure and should, if appropriate, be excluded.

Issued shares outstanding (in order to calculate market capitalization) – in the notes to the accounts. The note can usually be found from a reference in the consolidated balance sheet next to the heading "called-up share capital" or a similar term. The number of ordinary shares at the end of the year should be taken, and not their stated nominal money value (if any).

Share (stock) price (in order to calculate market capitalization) – from any daily newspaper or financial web site. Care should be taken to use the actual share price. Note also that financial newspapers often include individual companies' market capitalizations on their share price pages.

CALCULATING IT – THE THEORY

Figures 6.1a and 6.1b show the different numbers to be extracted from the accounts and how to use them to calculate the ratio.

Figure 6.1a Calculating the "Magic Number" for ... the PSR (half-yearly reporting)

Universal Widgets plc has a sales progression as follows:

(£m)	Jun-01	Six months to: Jun-00	Year to: Dec-00
Sales ...	120	100	200
It has issued shares of ...	200m		
... and a share price of ...	100p		
Last 12 months sales are ...	£220m		
(working)	(200 + 120 − 100)		
Market capitalization is ...	£200m		
(working)	200 × (100/100)		
PSR is ...	**0.91**		
(working)	(200/220)		

Figure 6.1b Calculating the "Magic Number" for ... the PSR (quarterly reporting)

Universal Widgets Inc. reports quarterly. Its quarterly pattern of sales is:

($m)	2000 Q1	2000 Q2	2000 Q3	2000 Q4	2001 Q1
Revenue ...	50	75	75	100	125
It has issued shares of ...	200m				
... and a stock price of ...	$10				
Last 12 months' sales are ...	$375m				
(working)	(75 + 75 + 100 + 125)				
Market capitalization is ...	$2,000m				
(working)	(200 × 10)				
PSR (or "revenue multiple") is ...	**5.3**				
(working)	(2,000/375)				

CALCULATING IT FOR SOLVAY

Figure 6.2 shows how the highlighted numbers extracted from the accounts of Solvay combine to produce the "magic number". More information on Solvay is available from *www.solvay.com*. Solvay is a leading Belgian pharmaceutical and chemical company. If you lose everything on the stock market you can access the "Depression Centre" at their site! Solvay is also number one in Europe and number two in the world for the manufacture of laxatives.

Figure 6.2 Calculating the PSR from Solvay's 1999 and Interim 2000 Accounts

The figures ...

Annual report 1999

Consolidated income statement summary (p. 61 in the published accounts of Solvay)

	1998 €m	1999 €m
Sales	7,451	**7,869**

Results for six months to June 2000 (p. 1)

	1999 €m	2000 €m
Sales	**3,725**	**4,600**
Number of shares in issue (000)	84,206	**84,314**
Solvay share price at time of writing	**€61.30**	

The calculation ...

PSR (based on last 12 months' sales) **0.59**

(working) (61.30 × 84,314/1,000)/(7,869 + 4,600 − 3,725)

Solvay's share price is multiplied by its shares in issue – the result expressed as millions – divided by last year's sales plus the difference between the sales in the current and last year's first half

In this instance, calculating the market capitalization is, as usual, straightforward. Refer back to "Magic number" 1. You must take care, however, to express the result in terms that are the same as those used to express the sales figure (millions comparing millions, and so on). This is a simple matter of adjusting decimal points to the common basis. Solvay's accounts and its half-yearly statement are admirably straightforward.

What it Means

Once somewhat unloved, the PSR has become increasingly and widely used as investors, or rather analysts and investment bankers, realized that it could be used to provide a valuation measure, however tenuous, for companies with no foreseeable outlook of making a profit.

Hence it has been used extensively to value Internet and telecoms companies, especially using forecasts of revenue rather than historically audited figures. As movements in the prices of some of these shares have shown, this has meant greater attention on whether or not these companies meet quarterly sales forecasts, and sharp downward movements in the stock price if they don't.

There is justification, as there is in the same way with PERs and earnings growth, for companies that can demonstrate high and consistent levels of sales revenue growth to sell on higher multiples of revenue than those whose sales are static or growing more slowly. This is far, however, from being a hard and fast rule.

For more mundane companies, PSR can be used as a way of assessing the cheapness or otherwise of the shares. The normal rule of thumb is simple. Companies that have a PSR of significantly less than one can be considered cheap: those that haven't are expensive.

There is a respectable body of evidence to suggest that this rule works.

In his book *What Works on Wall Street*, James O'Shaughnessy examined US share price and accounts data for an extended part of the post-war period and found that a historic PSR of less than one was the most reliable indicator of the future share price performance of companies.

EV/EBITDA

The Definition

EV/EBITDA is shorthand for a valuation method similar to the price-earnings ratio. It tries to gauge the value of the company by comparing one of the measures of its market value with a profit number derived from the income statement.

EV is "enterprise value". You can find out how to calculate it in "Magic number" 2.

EBITDA stands for "earnings before interest, tax, depreciation, and amortization". It is "operating income" or "operating profit" after adding back the charges for depreciation of fixed assets and amortization of goodwill. The reason for disregarding these charges is that they do not involve an actual cash expense.

The Formulas

EV/EBITDA = (Market capitalization + Net debt)/EBITDA

EBITDA = Pre-tax profit + Interest paid + Depreciation + Amortization

The Components

Enterprise value (see "Magic number" 2) has five elements:

Issued shares (common stock) outstanding – shares that have been issued and are publicly traded.

Share (stock) price – the current market price of the shares, normally the mid-market price at close of business on the previous trading day.

Multiply these two together to arrive at market capitalization. EV is market capitalization plus total debt minus cash.

Total debt – this is the total of long- and short-term debt issued by or owed by the company and its subsidiaries.

Cash – this is cash held at the company's bank and any liquid investments that can be turned into cash instantly.

EBITDA – this can be calculated with relative ease from information in the company's accounts. Most income statements (profit and loss accounts) follow a similar pattern, with sales at the top. The cost of materials and other external inputs is subtracted from this figure to arrive at gross profit. From gross profit various operating expenses are deducted – including some non-cash charges like depreciation of fixed assets and amortization (annual write-offs) of goodwill – to arrive at operating profit.

EBITDA is operating profit after adding back depreciation and amortization.

Where's the Data?

Enterprise value components

Issued shares (common stock) outstanding – in the notes to the accounts. The note can be found from a reference in the consolidated balance sheet next to the heading "called-up share capital" or a similar term. The number of ordinary shares at the end of the year should be taken.

Share (stock) price – from any daily newspaper or financial web site.

Total debt – from the consolidated (or "group") balance sheet under the heading "accounts receivable", "creditors", or "current liabilities" (for short-term debt), and further down the page for medium- and long-term loans.

Cash – from the consolidated (or "group") balance sheet, under the heading "current assets".

EBITDA components

Operating profit – in the main part of the income statement, usually immediately above the "interest" line.

Depreciation – normally taken from one of the first few notes to the accounts, under the heading "operating profit is taken after the following deductions", or "operating expenses include ..." Take the charge for the year, not the figure for accumulated depreciation (this is the total for several previous years). Depreciation is also usually given in the cash flow statement.

Amortization – this is sometimes stated separately in the income statement if it is a sizable figure, or alternatively in the notes alongside depreciation.

Calculating it – the Theory

Figure 7.1 shows the different numbers to be pulled from the accounts and how to use them to calculate the ratio.

Figure 7.1 Calculating the "Magic Number" for ... EV/EBITDA

Universal Widgets plc has:

Market capitalization of	£125m
Short-term debt of	£25m
Long-term debt of	£25m
Cash of	£10m
so EV (enterprise value) is	£165m
(working)	(125 + 25 + 25 − 10)
It has operating profit of	£10m
... fixed asset depreciation of	£2m
... and goodwill amortization of	£2.5m
EBITDA is	**£14.5m**
(working)	(10 + 2.0 + 2.5)
EV/EBITDA is	**11.4**
(working)	(165/14.5)

CALCULATING IT FOR

YAHOO!

Figure 7.2 shows how the highlighted numbers from this extract from the 1999 accounts of Yahoo! combine to produce the "magic number".

Figure 7.2 Calculating EV/EBITDA from Yahoo!'s 1999 Accounts

The figures ...		
(in thousands)	**Dec-31 1999**	**1998**
Consolidated statement of operations (p. 34 in the published accounts of Yahoo!)		
Net revenues	588,608	245,100
Gross profit	486,809	192,946
Income from operations	**66,733**	−13,721
Consolidated statement of cash flows (p. 36)		
Adjustments to reconcile net income to net cash		
Depreciation and amortization	**42,330**	16,472
Assets (p. 33)		
Current assets		
Cash and cash equivalents	**233,951**	230,961
Short-term investments	**638,508**	341,822
Stockholders' equity		
Preferred stock, $0.001 par value; 10,000 authorized, none issued or outstanding	0	0
Common stock, $0.001 par value; 900,000 authorized; **532,798** and 497,998 issued and outstanding respectively	533	498
Yahoo!'s share price at time of writing	**$57**	

The calculations ...

Market capitalization	**$30,369m**
(working)	(532,798,000 × 57)

Yahoo!'s 532.798 million shares are multiplied by the share price of $57

Enterprise value	**$29,496.54m**
(working)	(30,369.00 – 638.51 – 233.95)

Yahoo!'s market capitalization is less $638 million of short-term investments and $234 million of cash

EBITDA	**$109.06m**
(working)	(66.73 + 42.33)

Income from operations of $66.73 million to which is added back depreciation and amortization of $42.33 million

EV/EBITDA	**270.6**
(working)	(29,497/109)

Yahoo!'s EV of $29,496 million is divided by EBITDA of $109 million

Working out market capitalization and EV will soon become second nature. When using historic accounts data for the bottom half of the fraction, however, a particular problem becomes apparent: the figures quickly become out of date. This is especially so for those companies (such as Internet stocks) that really have to be valued on this basis alone. One alternative is to calculate EBITDA on a trailing 12 months' basis.

Coincidentally, part of the Yahoo! site (Yahoo! Finance at *http://finance.yahoo.com*) provides these figures in an easily digestible form. Typing in the ticker symbol YHOO for Yahoo!, and clicking on the item headed "profile" next to the price quote, takes you to a thumbnail sketch of Yahoo!'s business and finances. This includes a trailing 12 months' EBITDA figure, that, at the time of writing, was $315.4 million.

Since this is roughly three times the EBITDA figure arrived at by the calculation in the table using the historic accounts, checking out up-to-date numbers is very worthwhile. This would actually reduce the EV/EBITDA multiple to under 100 times, a somewhat less scary valuation. Sites where up-to-date accounting information can be found are outlined in the appendix.

What it Means

EV/EBITDA is used as a means of comparing companies with high levels of debt or lots of cash, or those that are making losses at the net income level but not necessarily further up the profit and loss column.

EV is a way of valuing a company in the same way, irrespective of its capital structure. Excluding the impact of interest and tax, by taking earnings before interest and tax (the EBIT in EBITDA) as the denominator of the fraction, balances this.

In other words, debt is added back on one side (in the EV calculation), and interest on debt is added back on the other side (in EBITDA). Also, using a pre-tax figure means that international differences in company tax rates can be ignored when comparing companies.

Is adding back charges like depreciation and amortization valid? The case is easier to make for amortization, especially where it is usually related to amortizing goodwill, an arbitrary policy recently introduced by accountants.

Those seeking to exclude depreciation from the equation are on shakier ground. Depreciation reflects the fact that physical assets wear out and have to be replaced.

Although it is a notional charge at the time it is made, depreciation is a marker for a real cost that must be borne by the business, and which will result in a cash expense in the future, when the assets are replaced.

Whether valid or not, this ratio is now widely used, but it needs to be treated with extreme care, especially where it is used to justify the stock market valuations of loss-making companies.

Price/Book Value

The Definition

Price/book value (P/BV) (often called "price to book") is the share price divided by the book value of the shares. Book value is the value of the net assets attributable to shareholders (alternatively called "net tangible assets", "shareholders' funds", or "stockholders' equity") expressed as a per-share figure.

The Formula

P/BV = Share price/(Shareholders' equity/Number of shares in issue)

The Components

Share (stock) price – the current market price of the shares, normally the mid-market price at close of business on the previous trading day.

Book value – this goes by a number of different names, including "stockholders' (or shareholders') equity", "shareholders' funds", "net assets", "net tangible assets", and so on. Take the figure that represents the tangible fixed assets of the business plus current assets, less current liabilities, long-term creditors, and provisions. The balance of these figures represents the residual assets that are "owned" by shareholders.

Issued shares (common stock) outstanding – shares that have been issued and are capable of being publicly traded. Use the shares outstanding at the point in time the calculation is performed for the calculation. These are normally obtained from the annual report but adjusted for any subsequent stock splits.

Where's the Data?

Share (stock) price – from any daily newspaper or financial web site. Take note of the units in which the share price is expressed. In the UK, shares are traditionally quoted in pence, so a market capitalization expressed in pounds must be adjusted accordingly.

Book value – on the face of the consolidated balance sheet normally using one of the alternative phrases listed earlier. It is also often represented by, and is identifiable as, the total of share capital and reserves.

Issued shares (common stock) outstanding – in the notes to the accounts. The note can be found from a reference in the consolidated balance sheet next to the heading "called-up share capital" or a similar term. The number of ordinary shares at the end of the year should be taken, and not their stated nominal money value (if any).

The number of shares used to calculate earnings per share should not be used. This will normally be an average for the year, not the most recent figure. In this instance, the most recent figure is the one to use.

Calculating it – the Theory

Figure 8.1 shows the different numbers to be pulled from the accounts and how to use them to calculate the ratio.

Figure 8.1 Calculating the "Magic Number" for ... Price/Book Value

Universal Widgets has:

A share price of	200p
Shareholders' equity of	£600m
Shares outstanding of	400m
Book value per share is	150p
(working)	(600/400) × 100
Price to book is	**1.33**
(working)	(200/150)

Calculating it for NTT

Figure 8.2 shows how the highlighted numbers from this extract from the accounts of NTT combine to produce the "magic number".

Figure 8.2 Calculating Price/Book Value from NTT's 2000 Accounts

The figures ...

(in million ¥)	**Mar-31 1999**	**2000**
Shareholders' equity (p. 39 in the published accounts of NTT)		
Common stock, ¥50,000 par value; Authorised 62,400,000 shares Issued and oustanding – 15,912,000 shares in 1999 **15,834,590** shares in 2000	795,600	795,600
Additional paid-in capital	2,530,476	2,530,476
Retained earnings	2,628,272	2,648,286
Accumulated other income (loss)	−43,578	40,262
	5,910,770	**6,014,624**
NTT's share price at time of writing	**¥900,000**	

The calculations ...

Book value per share is **¥379,831**
(working) (6,014,624/15.835 to both figures with millions omitted)

NTT's shareholders' equity is divided by shares in issue of 15,835 million

Price to book value is **2.37**
(working) (900,000/379,831)

NTT's share price is divided by the book value per share figure from the previous calculation

As in the earlier example of enterprise value (EV), NTT's accounts are clear when it comes to extracting the information, the main problem being that of dealing with the numbers themselves. Because of NTT's heavyweight share price, these are cumbersome.

Although the calculation is straightforward, elsewhere in NTT's balance sheet there are two items that might give rise to an adjustment to the book value figure.

The first is a substantial one, of ¥1882 billion, related to intangible assets. Checking in the appropriate note to the accounts shows that two-thirds of this amount relates to the value of computer software, and the remainder to rights to use utility facilities.

Whether or not you exclude this from the calculation might depend on whether similar items were included in the accounts of, say, other telecoms companies with which you wish to compare NTT. If so, it is a fairly simple matter to deduct the intangible amount from the stockholders' equity figure, and work out a new book value per share figure and a new price to book ratio.

The same is true of the company's investment in marketable securities. These are carried in the balance sheet at market value; that is, with unrealized gains and losses included. However, the amount involved – ¥120 billion difference between this and the book cost of these investments, found in the relevant note to the accounts – is fairly small.

Taking these two items together, however, would reduce NTT's book value by ¥2,000 billion. This reduces NTT's book value from ¥6 trillion to ¥4 trillion in round figures. Book value per share goes down to ¥253,426, and, since the share price remains the same at ¥900,000, the effect of this adjustment is to raise the price to book value to 3.55 times.

What it Means

Opinions differ about how book value should be calculated. For the purposes of this calculation, most definitions exclude minority interests (the proportion of assets in partly owned subsidiaries that is owned by outside shareholders) and goodwill.

Another issue of definition relates to the value placed on property assets and listed and unlisted investments. The most common convention is that long-term property assets can be included on the basis of an annual revaluation, and that listed investments can be included at cost or market value, and unlisted investments at cost. These distinctions are most important when using "price to book" as a tool for comparing different companies.

In NTT's case, as explained above, the company currently includes intangible assets and listed investments at market value as part of shareholders' equity. Excluding these items makes a material difference to the calculation.

While "price to book" is a widely used quick yardstick, it needs interpreting with care, and not just because of the quirks of calculation explained above. The more serious objection to it is that, while it works well for companies that are rich in tangible assets, it is less meaningful for those that have substantial elements of goodwill or intellectual property in their balance sheets.

What matters more is not where the share price stands in relation to assets, but the profits management generates from the assets at its disposal. Return on assets is much more relevant to the long-term value of a company as an investment. We return to this theme later in "Magic numbers" 19 and 20.

Part Two

Income Statement "Magic Numbers"

Income Statement "Magic Numbers"

The four ratios included in this part are solely derived from the income statement.

Income statement "magic numbers" allow you to get a more in-depth view of the cost structure of the business and how it affects profitability. Costs can be external, generated inside the company, or related to finance.

Earnings per share and dividends per share have already cropped up in Part One. Part Two highlights the complexities that sometimes occur when calculating them, how to interpret the numbers, and how they interact with each other.

Profit and loss (P&L) account "magic numbers" can have a more subtle influence on share prices than is true for the market-based ratios described earlier.

- Margin calculations (the percentage of profit to sales) have a key bearing on understanding the company's business and how it functions on a daily basis. There are three types of margin calculation examined later.
- Interest cover (the ratio of pre-interest profits to the cost of finance) is an important variable. It has an impact on profitability, especially when the direction of interest rates is changing. Interest cover measures can affect your choice of companies to invest in, and those to avoid.
- Earnings per share and dividend per share calculations are more complex than they might seem at first sight. It is important to be able to calculate them accurately to make valid comparisons between companies.
- Dividend cover (the degree to which the cash dividend payment is exceeded by earnings per share) is a crucial variable. It is particularly useful when comparing companies that pay out high levels of income to shareholders, or those that generate high returns.

How should we interpret these numbers? Things are not often as straightforward as they seem.

Take margins first. More important than the absolute level of margins is the trend in them over time. Margins vary with the nature of the business – food retail companies have low margins; software companies have high ones. It is more important to compare the trend in margins over several years, and the margins recorded by different companies in the same industry.

Interest cover is important, but it needs to be combined with an analysis of the nature of the loans and other borrowings giving rise to the interest charge.

It might be worth buying highly geared shares, which will normally have a low interest cover, if interest rates are set to fall. But this will be true only if they stand to benefit from the fall in rates in a demonstrable way, perhaps because their debt is at variable rates.

Calculating earnings and dividends accurately is the basis for correctly calculating the price-earnings and PEG ratios that featured in Part One. Comparing earnings trends and growth rates, or cyclical patterns in earnings between companies in the same industry, can yield valuable insights – but accounting distortions must be stripped out.

Dividend cover calculations are crucial for "income shares" that are bought primarily because they have a large dividend yield.

Cover is one way of sifting between shares with similar income characteristics. If cover is lower, the income from the shares is possibly less secure and may be reduced at some future date.

What goes unsaid in this instance, and is beyond the scope of "magic numbers," is the extent to which politics comes into the equation. Dividend cuts sometimes occur because new management brooms enter a company, to make a policy point to government, or to soften the blow of a plant closure if it can be pointed out that shareholders are suffering too.

As a result, the qualitative factors need watching as sharply as the quantitative ones.

As in the previous part, the pages that follow examine each of the next four "magic numbers" in more depth. Read further to find out how to get the data you need, how to calculate them, and what they mean.

We have again used real-life examples and extracts from the actual accounts of companies in different parts of the world to demonstrate the calculations in practice.

Remember, however, that the income statement is the least reliable part of a company's accounts, and the one where management has the most leeway to manipulate the figures. Keep your eyes open for inconsistencies. If the figures look too good to be true, they probably are!

Margins

The Definition

For *margins*, read "profit margins". In general terms, these are measures of profitability found by dividing a profit figure by sales revenue. The profit and loss account (or income statement) contains several different measures of profit. So, in turn, there are several ways of calculating margins. These are:

Gross margin – the percentage that gross profit represents of sales revenue.

Operating margin – the percentage that operating profit represents of sales revenue.

Pre-tax margin – the percentage that profit before tax represents of sales revenue.

The Formulas

Gross margin = (Gross profit × 100)/Sales revenue

Operating margin = (Operating profit × 100)/Sales revenue)

Pre-tax margin = (Pre-tax profit × 100)/Sales revenue

The Components

Sales – "sales", "revenue", and "turnover" are virtually interchangeable terms and are in such common use as to need little further explanation. Calculations can differ in whether or not you take the sales for the last reported year, or for the last 12 months. The latter may include sales for half-years or quarters that have elapsed since the previous financial year-end. See "Magic number" 6 for more detail on this.

Margins can be calculated for part of a year – provided that the profit figure for a particular period is compared with the sales figure for the same period.

Gross profit – imagine that the income statement is a column that starts with sales, from which items are deducted successively to arrive at different levels of profit, the bottom-most item being retained profit. Gross profit is always the top-most profit figure quoted in the income statement (although some accounts omit it altogether, proceeding directly to operating profit – see below). Gross profit is normally defined as sales revenue minus the cost of sales. "Cost of sales" means the cost of any bought-in raw materials or components.

Operating profit – sometimes called "operating income", this is the next level down in the profit "column" and is found by taking gross profit and deducting various other items. These include depreciation and amortization, staff costs, and sales and marketing expenditure. Not deducted, at least until the next stage, is income (or losses) attributable to related companies (companies that are less than 50% owned), or net interest paid or received.

Pre-tax profit – this is operating income after deducting (or crediting as appropriate) any remaining items down to, but not including, tax.

Where's the Data?

Sales – normally the top-most figure or subtotal in the consolidated profit and loss account or income statement.

Gross profit – if calculated separately this is also found in the income statement below the sales (turnover, or revenue) figure.

Operating profit – this is found a little further down the income statement and is occasionally called "trading profit", although there are some subtle accounting distinctions between the two. Trading profit tends to correspond to profit before interest (sometimes called EBIT – earnings before interest and tax) and may include items; say, the profit on sales of fixed asset investments – that do not relate directly to the mainstream operations of the company.

Pre-tax profit – this is in the income statement immediately above the tax line. It is a matter of debate whether or not you include non-trading or extraordinary items. If you exclude items like this from profit, then you must also exclude the revenue relating to them from the sales figure you use to calculate margins.

Calculating it – the Theory

Figure 9.1 shows the different numbers to be extracted from the accounts and how to use them to calculate the ratio.

Figure 9.1 Calculating the "Magic Number" for ... Margins

Universal Widgets has an income statement that looks like this:

Year to 31 December	**2000**
	£m
Turnover	200
less: Cost of sales	60
Gross profit	140
less: Operating expenses	70
Operating profit	70
less: Interest paid	20
Pre-tax profit	50
less: Taxation	20
Profit after tax	30
less: Minority interests	2
Profit attributable to shareholders	28
less: Dividends	8
Retained profits	20
Gross margin is	**70%**
(working)	(140 × 100)/200
Operating margin is	**35%**
(working)	(70 × 100)/200
Pre-tax margin is	**25%**
(working)	(50 × 100)/200

CALCULATING IT FOR GREAT UNIVERSAL STORES

Figure 9.2 shows how the highlighted numbers from this extract from the accounts of GUS combine to produce the "magic numbers".

Figure 9.2 Calculating Margins from GUS's 2000 Accounts

The figures ...

Year to 31 March (p. 42 in the published accounts of GUS)	**2000 £m**	**1999 £m**
Turnover – continuing operations	**5,658.4**	5,466.6
Cost of sales	−3,436.1	−3,260.3
Gross profit	**2,222.3**	2,206.3
Net operating expenses	−1,801.6	−1,668.3
Operating profit – continuing operations	**420.7**	538.0
Share of operating profit of JV	33.9	31.9
Related companies	11.3	22.1
Profit on sale of fixed assets	11.1	0.0
Trading profit	477.0	592.0
Loss on termination of business	0.0	−14.3
Profit before interest	477.0	577.7
less: Interest paid	−97.4	−127.3
Pre-tax profit	**379.6**	450.4
less: Taxation	−104.5	−127.4
Profit after tax	275.1	323.0
less: Dividends	207.2	207.2
Retained profits	67.9	115.8

The calculations ...

Gross margin **39.3%**
(working) (2,222.3 × 100)/5,658.4

GUS's gross profit of £2,222.3 million is divided by a turnover of £5,658.4 million and the result expressed as a percentage

Operating margin **7.4%**
(working) (420.7 × 100)/5,658.4

GUS's operating profit of £420.7 million is divided by a turnover of £5658.4 million and the result expressed as a percentage

Pre-tax margin **6.7%**
(working) (379.6 × 100)/5,658.4

GUS's pre-tax profit of £379.6 million is divided by turnover of £5,658.4 million and the result expressed as a percentage

GUS's accounts are remarkably straightforward when it comes to calculating these numbers. One tricky point, however, is whether or not the profit on sale of fixed asset investments and the loss on termination of business should be excluded. The reason is that their inclusion would distort comparison between the two years.

More detail is given in the notes to the accounts. These show the revenue relating to the sale of fixed asset investments to be £15.7 million (on which the profit was £11.1 million). The loss on termination of business relates to closure costs. By their nature, they have no revenue attached. Adjusting for the sales of fixed asset investments (that is, deducting £15.7 million from sales, and £11.1 million from profits) reduces the pre-tax margin by 0.2 percentage points.

What it Means

Margins are important indicators of the health of a business. They are at their most revealing when comparisons are made either between companies, or over an extended period of time (say, five financial years) at the same company. This allows the all-important trend in margins to be established.

What should you look for? In short, margins that are either steady or rising gently. Falling margins can be a sign of problems, especially if the company or the industry involved is not cyclical. This is because margin numbers show the extent to which the company is able to pass on bought-in costs in its prices to customers (its gross margin), and the extent to which it has its own internal costs under control (its operating margin).

Gross margins are also an indicator of value added – the higher the gross margin, the more value the company itself is adding to raw materials and bought-in inputs.

GUS is a quasi-retail business involved in both branded high street and mail-order retailing. Retailers are often judged on their margin performance. Food retailers, which depend on high throughput of goods and keen prices, operate on low margins. They offset this by taking money from customers at the checkout much faster than they pay their suppliers. Software companies, which license their intellectual property and have limited bought-in costs, have high gross margins.

Magic Number

10 Interest Cover

The Definition

Interest cover (sometimes referred to as "income-gearing") is a measure of the financial soundness of a company. It is the number of times by which profit before interest exceeds the interest charge in the income statement.

The Formula

Interest cover = (Pre-tax profit + Net interest paid)/Net interest paid

The Components

Pre-tax profit – this is operating income after deducting (or crediting as appropriate) items such as income from related companies (companies that are less than 50% owned), net interest paid or received, special charges, and any other items down to – but not including – tax.

Net interest paid – this is the interest paid on the company's outstanding bank debt or bonds minus any interest earned on cash balances and short-term liquid investments.

The amount of interest paid as stated in the income statement may not always equate precisely to the interest paid in cash terms by the company.

For example, bond interest may be paid once or twice yearly in big lumps. Normally, a company will be allowed to include an estimate of the proportion that has accrued during the period in question.

Interest is also sometimes capitalized. This means it is taken out of the income statement and counted in the balance sheet. This is normally done where interest is paid on financing for a project that has yet to be completed but that is expected to have a long-term value to the company once completed. An example is interest on finance relating to constructing property such as retail stores.

Treating interest payments as capital items reduces the charge taken in the income statement and hence boosts profits. But it does not alter the fact that the cash amount of interest due still has to be paid.

Where's the Data?

Pre-tax profit – this is found in the income statement immediately above the tax line. As with margins, it is a matter of debate whether or not one should include non-trading or extraordinary items as part of pre-tax profit when calculating interest cover. If the items are sizable credits that may not recur, it is better to exclude them from the calculation.

Net interest paid – this is found in the income statement above the pre-tax profit line and above any non-trading or extraordinary items. It may not be obvious, or stated overtly, whether or not interest has been capitalized. It is always worth consulting the notes to the accounts relating to the interest item to discover if there has been a reduction in the interest paid item in the income statement on this score.

Calculating it – the Theory

Figure 10.1 shows the different numbers to be pulled from the accounts and how to use them to calculate the ratio.

Figure 10.1 Calculating the "Magic Number" for ... Interest Cover

Universal Widgets Inc. has:

Pre-tax profit of	$10m
Net interest paid of	$2.5m
Notes to the accounts show capitalized interest of	$1m
Pre-tax profit less capitalized interest is	$9m
Interest cover excluding capitalized interest is	**5.0 times**
(working)	(10.0 + 2.5)/2.5
Interest cover including capitalized interest is	**3.6 times**
(working)	(9.0 + 3.5)/3.5

CALCULATING IT FOR
McDONALD'S

Figure 10.2 shows how the highlighted numbers from this extract from the accounts of McDonald's combine to produce the "magic number". McDonald's (more information is available from their web site at *www.mcdonalds.com*) is an American global food service retailer. The company serves 43 million people a day in 120 countries.

Figure 10.2 Calculating Interest Cover from McDonald's 1999 Accounts

The figures ...

Year to 31 December ($m)	**1999**	**1998**	**1997**
Consolidated statement of income (p. 25 in the published accounts of McDonald's)			
Operating income	3,319.6	2,761.9	2,808.3
Interest expense – net of capitalized interest of $**14.3**, 17.9, and 22.7	**396.3**	413.8	364.4
Non-operating expense	39.2	40.7	36.6
Income before provision for income taxes	**2,884.1**	2,307.4	2,407.4

The calculations ...

Interest cover excluding capitalized interest	**8.3**
(working)	(2,884.1 + 396.3)/396.3

McDonald's income before taxes plus interest expense is divided by the interest expense

Interest cover including capitalized interest	**8.0**
(working)	(2,884.1 + 396.3)/(396.3 + 14.3)

McDonald's income before taxes plus interest expense is divided by the interest expense plus capitalized interest

McDonald's is commendably open about the fact that it capitalizes a relatively modest proportion of its interest bill. The figure presumably represents the interest cost incurred in developing new restaurants prior to their opening. The result is that interest cover, whether including and excluding this, does not change much.

Another point about the two alternative calculations is that the capitalized interest item needs only to be added back to the numerator to work out interest cover allowing for capitalized interest. Pre-interest profit is the same irrespective of whether or not capitalized interest is included.

What it Means

Interest cover is an important number in two or three respects. In the first place, interest cover is one of the key variables monitored by lenders and bondholders. Bond issues frequently contain clauses (covenants) that provide for penalties if interest cover drops below a certain figure.

Interest cover can also be a proxy for how sensitive or otherwise the business is to changes in interest rates. This requires investigation of the type of debt that produces the company's interest bill. If a large proportion of debt is variable rates, the interest charge could drop significantly as interest rates drop, producing a gain in pre-tax profits.

Interest cover is also a general indicator of corporate robustness. A low level of interest cover might mean that a company's competitors would conclude (as might its investors) that it was in no position to withstand a period of aggressive price competition that would reduce profits.

While a certain level of debt, and therefore interest payments, can provide gearing and enhance shareholder returns in an inherently stable business, it can also be a drawback if a company goes through a bad patch, which will exaggerate the extent of any underlying downturn in profits.

Finally, interest cover has little practical significance if a company has net cash in its balance sheet and hence no net interest paid.

Earnings per Share

The Definition

The *earnings per share* (EPS) calculation is a key component of several other "magic numbers". It is net profit attributable to ordinary shareholders divided by the weighted average of shares in issue during the period in question.

The Formula

EPS = Net profit attributable/Weighted average shares in issue

The Components

Weighted average shares in issue – the time-weighted average number of shares in issue during the year. The shares concerned are those that have been issued and publicly listed.

Occasionally, earnings per share calculations are based around what are called "fully diluted" issued shares outstanding. This takes in the extra shares that may be issued in the future; for example, as a result of the exercise of executive share options.

Any stock splits should also be taken into account. The calculation of the weighted average is normally performed on a monthly basis. As an example, an increase in shares in issue that took place eight months into the year would mean that the total shares issued after the increase took place would have a weighting of 4/12 while the original shares in issue would have a weighting of 8/12.

WHERE'S THE DATA?

Net profit attributable – this is normally found at the very bottom of the income statement, in the line immediately above the one that states the cost of ordinary dividends.

Weighted average shares in issue – this is generally found in the notes to the accounts referred to by the earnings per share line in the income statement. Earnings per share are, however, often calculated for investors and stated at the foot of the income statement. The note will normally say what weighted average number has been used in the calculation.

Occasionally, earnings per share are stated on a "fully diluted" basis. This is based on the shares in issue on the assumption that all outstanding share options are exercised and, if they exist, any convertible preference shares or convertible bonds are converted. In the latter case, any deductions relating to convertible instruments – such as convertible bond interest or convertible preference share dividends – should be adjusted for tax if necessary and added back to net profit before the calculation is performed.

CALCULATING IT – THE THEORY

Figure 11.1 shows the different numbers to be pulled from the accounts and how to use them to calculate the ratio.

Figure 11.1 Calculating the "Magic Number" for ... Earnings per Share

Universal Widgets plc has:

Profits after tax of	£7.5m
Minority interests of	£0.5m
Preference dividends of	£0.2m
Shares in issue at the start of the year	20m
Shares added at end of August	4m
Shares at 31 December	24m
Attributable profits are	£6.8m
(working)	(7.5 − 0.5 − 0.2)
Weighted average shares in issue are	21.333m
(working)	(8/12 × 20) + (4/12 × 24)
Earnings per share are	**31.9p**
(working)	(6.8/21.333) × 100

CALCULATING IT FOR RWE

Figure 11.2 shows how the highlighted numbers from this extract from the accounts of the German utility company RWE combine to produce the "magic number". More information on the company is at *www.rwe.com.*

Figure 11.2 Calculating Earnings per Share from RWE's 2000 Accounts

The figures ...

Consolidated income statement year ended 30 June (p. 98 in the published accounts of RWG)	**2000 (€m)**	**1999 (€m)**
Profit before tax	2,151	2,722
Taxes on income	595	1,177
Profit after tax	1,556	1,545
Minority interest	344	396
Net profit	**1,212**	**1,149**
Note 23 (p. 129)		
Net profit (€m)	**1,212**	**1,149**
Dividend per share (€)	1.00	1.00
Number of shares outstanding (weighted average, in thousands)	**541,545**	**555,251**

The calculation ...

Earnings per share (in €)	**2.24**	**2.07**
(working ... in millions)	(1,212/541,545)	(1,149/555,251)

In each case, RWE's net profit is divided by the weighted average number of shares in issue in the same year

While this calculation appears simple, RWE states in the notes to the accounts, that it has preference shares outstanding, and that it calculates earnings per share based on taking the two classes of shares (preference and ordinary) together as if there were no difference between them.

It is not possible to work out, from the accounts alone, whether there is a dividend payable on the preference shares. The note relating to earnings per share appears to imply that any differences between the two classes of share relate to voting rights, rather than any preferential allocation of dividends. Hence, the two classes of share are taken together when working out weighted average shares in issue.

The reduction in weighted average capital evident in the calculation is the result of a substantial proportion of the preference shares having been repurchased by the company in the course of the year.

Similarly, the note alludes to the possibility of dilution from stock options and convertible bonds. Calculations for this are not provided, although it is asserted that the diluted earnings per share figures would not be significantly different.

What it Means

Earnings per share calculations are a key measure of corporate performance in many instances, but it is unwise to use them in isolation. One reason is that accounting policies differ between companies and between countries. It is sometimes hard to work out whether or not one is comparing like with like.

Profits are also capable of manipulation to produce a smooth and eye-catching upward-pointing curve. Slight changes to depreciation policies, the inclusion of property profits, capitalizing interest, and buying in shares can all be used to influence the earnings per share figure. So just taking an earnings figure at face value can be a mistake.

There are also differences of opinion about how to treat the effects of dilution. Convertible bonds are frequently only convertible at a specified time in the future. Even if they are convertible now, they will only be converted if the present level of the underlying share price makes it attractive for holders to do so. Hence, if the share price is way below the conversion price, dilution is more theoretical than likely.

My own preference is to use diluted earnings if the company is in the conversion period and to use it even if the share price is at a level that would not encourage it to take place. If a convertible bond has not yet entered the conversion period, use undiluted earnings.

Taking earnings diluted for share options is realistic, provided the options are likely to be exercised in the near future, or the dilution effect is particularly large.

Common sense is also needed. Earnings growth is a key measure, but when calculating a company's earnings for several successive years, or when comparing different companies, make sure that all of the calculations are carried out on the same basis.

Magic Number

12

Dividend Cover

The Definition

Dividend cover is the number of times the dividend to shareholders (stockholders) is covered by profits attributable to shareholders.

The Formulas

Dividend cover = Earnings per share/Dividend per share

or

$$\text{Dividend cover} = \frac{\text{Net profit attributable to ordinary shareholder}}{\text{Cost of dividend paid in the year}}$$

The Components

Net income – profit attributable to shareholders after deducting tax and minority interests. Minority interests are the profits to be apportioned to other shareholders in subsidiaries that are less than 100% owned. Using fully diluted earnings per share in a dividend cover calculation is unduly hypothetical. If in doubt, the best course of action is to use actual, rather than per-share, amounts.

Issued shares (common stock) outstanding – shares that have been issued and are publicly listed. This includes shares that are "tightly held" by directors and their families, even though these may rarely change hands.

For earnings per share calculations it is normal to use "weighted average" shares in issue. As explained earlier, this calculates the average number of shares in issue during the period when the profit was being earned, giving due weight to extra shares issued during the period according to the time they were issued. Shares issued at the beginning of the year carry more weight than those issued toward the end. See "Magic number" 11 for more detail on this concept. If in doubt, use actual, rather than per-share, numbers.

Cost of dividend – this is normally included in the accounts and calculated as the per-share dividend for the year as a whole multiplied by the number of shares ranking for the dividend. The actual cash dividend paid in that particular year may be a different figure, because the payment date for the final dividend payment declared for the year will only be known when the full-year results are declared, and that will be after the company's year-end.

Where's the Data?

Net income – this is found in the profit and loss account (income statement), normally at the bottom of the page. Profit earned for ordinary shareholders (stockholders) should be used; namely, the figure before any ordinary dividend payments are deducted.

Earnings per share – normally stated separately and immediately below the net income figure. If there is a dilution factor arising from the likely future issue of new shares – for example, as a result of the exercising of executive share options – the earnings per share allowing for this factor may also be separately stated. If small, this figure can be disregarded for the purposes of the calculation of dividend cover.

Issued shares (or common stock) outstanding – detailed earnings per share calculations are normally given in a note to the accounts referred to from the income statement. The note should explicitly state the weighted average shares issued used in the calculation.

Cost of dividends – this is normally given in the income statement immediately below the figure for net profit attributable to stockholders. If not, it will almost certainly be contained in a note to the accounts, which should also state the per-share amounts of dividends paid. In both cases, the figures to use are the net cost to the company and the amount received by the stockholder, disregarding any notional tax deductions.

Dividends per share and earnings per share for the year are normally also included in the financial highlights or the five-year summary of trading that many companies include in their accounts. Using these figures can simplify calculating dividend cover.

CALCULATING IT – THE THEORY

Figure 12.1 shows the different numbers to be pulled from the accounts and how to use them to calculate the ratio.

Figure 12.1 Calculating the "Magic Number" for ... Dividend Cover

Singapore Widgets Pte has:

Profit attributable to shareholders of	$50m
Cost of dividend of	$15m
Shares in issue at the beginning and end of the year of	10.0m
Earnings per share are therefore	$5
Dividend per share is	$1.5
Dividend cover is	**3.33 times**
(working)	(5/1.5 or 50/15)

CALCULATING IT FOR
CHUGOKU ELECTRIC POWER

Figure 12.2 shows how the highlighted numbers from this extract from the accounts of Chugoku Electric Power (more information at *www.energia.co.jp*) combine to produce the "magic number".

Figure 12.2 Calculating Dividend Cover from Chugoku Electric Power's 2000 Accounts

The figures ...

Consolidated statements of income		**¥ (millions)**	
Years ended 31 March	**2000**	**1999**	**1998**
(p. 24 in the published accounts of Chugoko Electric Power)			
Income before minority interests	27,633	29,205	30,214
Minority interests	−18	101	−51
Net income	**27,615**	29,306	30,163
Per share data (note 2)			
Net income (basic)	**¥74.43**	78.98	81.29
Net income (diluted)	73.88	78.32	80.57
Cash dividends applicable to the year	**60.00**	50.00	50.00

	¥ (millions)
Consolidated statement of cash flow (p. 26)	**2,000**
Cash flows used in financing activities:	
Cash dividends paid	**−18,529**

The calculations ...

Dividend cover (calculated by per share method) **1.24**
(working) (74.43/60.00)

Chugoku's basic net income per share is divided by the dividend for the year

Dividend cover (calculated by using actual money amounts) **1.49**
(working) (27,615/18,529)

Chugoku's net income of ¥27.615 billion is divided by the cash cost of the dividend of ¥18.5 billion taken from the cash flow statement

Figure 12.2 highlights some of the problems that can be encountered when calculating dividend cover. The first calculation is the conventional earnings per share divided by the dividend per share. Although there is an earnings dilution factor present, it is small and can be ignored.

Using the actual money amounts demonstrates how the calculations can differ. Chugoku's accounts do not appear to disclose the actual projected cost of the dividend for the year to March 2000. Calculating the ratio using the cost of dividend from the cash flow statement produces a more generous figure for cover.

This is because the cash cost recorded in the year will be the final payment from the previous year and the interim payment for the year to March 2000. Because the dividend in this case increased from one year to the next, the cash cost in the year will be less than the amount that subsequently was paid in respect of the year to March 2000.

What it Means

Dividend cover is an important measure for assessing stocks that are bought for the dividend income they yield, and for assessing whether it is likely or not that the dividend payment might be cut in the immediate future.

When assessing high-yield shares, therefore, dividend cover becomes an important indicator of the security of the return. A share with a dividend yield of 7% and a cover of 1.5 might be considered a safer bet than one with a dividend yield of 8% but a dividend cover of only 1.1.

Whether or not minimally covered dividends are maintained or cut is also a good indication of management's view of the prospects for profit growth in the following year. The decision on the final dividend payment for the year is often made three months or so into the new financial year, by which time management may have some indication of which way the wind is blowing.

In growth stocks, by contrast, investors use dividend cover from the opposite standpoint: as a way of calculating the level of profits that are retained in the business for future investment. This is important, especially when management has the knack of generating high returns from the assets of the business. The more those assets can be enlarged through retaining profits, the greater the potential future returns.

Many high-growth companies do not pay dividends at all, and not just because, in some cases, they do not make profits. For high-return, high-growth companies, it makes more sense to retain profits than to pay them out to shareholders.

Part Three

Balance Sheet "Magic Numbers"

Balance Sheet "Magic Numbers"

When times are good, many investors pay little attention to the balance sheets of the companies they invest in. This is a mistake. Times change, and what can seem a sound company when the weather is fair may turn out to be very vulnerable when storm clouds gather.

When times get really bad, a company is often only worth what its assets can be sold for. Assets in such a situation might include the intangible worth of staff, brand names, order books, and business contacts, but these are hard to measure. What is the price of a failed dot.com business with no unique selling point and no staff?

This section concentrates largely on what can be measured and how best to use the information.

Using the "magic numbers" available to analyze the balance sheet also works well with companies that are, by convention, valued on the basis of their assets rather than their profits. These include property companies and some retailers, which may be property companies in disguise, investment companies, and insurance groups.

Beware of those who say that times have changed and balance sheets no longer matter. That is simply the first sign of a gathering storm.

Remember, however, that although they are vital to understanding companies, balance sheets take some investigating. Companies differ in the way they account for particular items, and some of the important information may be buried in the notes to the accounts and hard to get at. That said, accounting policies relating to balance sheets are becoming more standardized and more transparent. Country-by-country differences are being ironed out, though this process is still incomplete.

The "magic numbers" outlined in these pages will help you to ferret out the true worth of a company and cut through the misleading gloss.

These are the ways balance sheet "magic numbers" can help you.

- The current ratio and the acid ratio allow you to examine the short-term resources of the company (or its lack of them).
- Debtor and creditor days allow you to see how quickly a company is collecting money from its customers, and how quickly it is paying its suppliers.
- Stock days tell you how efficient the company is at turning over its stock.
- Gearing tells you how the borrowings of the company compare with its assets and whether or not the company is vulnerable to changes in interest rates.
- Price/cash shows you how much cash backs up the share price. This is important when times are tough.
- The burn rate tells you how quickly a loss-making company will exhaust its cash reserves. This has come into its own as a means of assessing Internet companies.
- Return on capital shows you how much management is able to generate from all of the capital at its disposal, both equity and debt.
- Return on equity measures how productively management is using the capital contributed by equity shareholders. This is a critical ratio for evaluating a growth company.
- Net asset value (NAV) is a per-share measure of the worth of the underlying assets of the company, but it can be calculated in several different ways.
- Premium or discount to NAV represents where the price stands in relation to this figure, and is often used to evaluate investment companies and large property groups.

Even more than with some of the earlier numbers, not all of these "magic numbers" are of equal importance in every company, but each is an essential element in the box of tools at investors' disposal.

Debtor and creditor days and stock turnover are critical for businesses that buy in and process raw materials from outside, or who rely on efficient selling to generate profits. Clearly, debtor days (how fast your customers pay you) are irrelevant for "cash" businesses, since money is handed over immediately.

Gearing is not especially relevant if a company has minimal debt, but should always be investigated. Burn rate is a vital tool for assessing loss-making companies and should be calculated every time new financial information is produced, to monitor how it is changing.

Return on equity is a vital way of measuring how growth stocks are likely to perform, and it is a key part of a ratio we will look at later. However, care needs to be taken to calculate it properly.

Net asset value, and where the stock price stands relative to it, is important for certain types of company. For some, especially those with hard-to-measure intangible assets, it is more difficult to calculate and use.

The sections that follow examine each of the ten balance sheet "magic numbers" in depth. Now read on …

Magic Number

13 Current Ratio and Acid Ratio

The Definition

These are two ratios that assess a company's short-term liquidity.

The *current ratio* compares current assets (normally stocks, debtors – money owed by customers – and cash) with current liabilities. Current liabilities include bank overdrafts, money the company owes to suppliers and the tax authorities, and other payments that might have to be made at short notice.

The acid test ratio (sometimes abbreviated to *acid ratio*) is largely the same as the current ratio, but excludes stocks from current assets. This is done because, in an extreme situation, stocks may not be sold for their full price.

The Formulas

Current ratio = Current assets/Current liabilities

Acid ratio = (Current assets − Stocks)/Current liabilities

The Components

Current assets – typically, stocks (or inventory), debtors (accounts receivable), and cash. Stocks are defined separately below.

Debtors (*accounts receivable, or simply "receivables"*) – represents the money owed to the company by its customers.

Cash – this item speaks for itself.

Current assets sometimes include short-term investments. To qualify as current assets they must be highly marketable securities (such as short-term government bonds or money-market instruments). This means they will vary little in price in the short term and can be quickly sold and turned into cash.

Stocks (*sometimes called inventory*) – this refers to unsold finished goods or those still in the process of being made. The definition sometimes expands, for companies involved in long-term contracts, to include the value of work-in-progress for which customers have not yet been invoiced.

Controlling the level of inventory is vital to a business's health. Stocks represent products that can be turned into cash. Too much stock means that capital is being tied up unnecessarily. For businesses in difficulty, or those selling fashion items, unsold stock may not be as liquid as it appears, or at least not at a "normal" price. To turn it into cash may necessitate deep discounts being offered to tempt buyers.

Current liabilities – now called, in UK accounting parlance, "creditors due within one year". The term is a "catch all" for a number of disparate items. These include: short-term bank borrowings and other debt repayable within a year; money owed to suppliers (accounts payable); liabilities due to government agencies, such as tax payments, VAT, and other items; and dividends to shareholders. Few of these payments can be postponed for long without the company running into trouble.

Where's the Data?

Current assets – this item is found in the consolidated balance sheet, normally immediately under the items relating to fixed assets. Expanded details of the individual components are normally contained in the notes to the accounts.

Stocks – this is part of the "current" assets group, in the consolidated balance sheet. Expanded details on stocks (inventory) may also be in the note to the accounts relating to current assets. A guide to the way in which the stock values have been reached may also be in the note about significant accounting policies.

Current liabilities – this is also in the consolidated balance sheet, normally immediately below the current assets item. The term "current liabilities" may be used, or "short-term creditors", or "creditors due within one year".

Calculating it – the Theory

Figure 13.1 shows the different numbers to be pulled from the accounts and how to use them to calculate the ratio.

Figure 13.1 Calculating the "Magic Number" for ... Current Ratio/Acid Ratio

Universal Widgets plc has current assets and current liabilities that look like this:

	£m
Current assets	
Stocks	20
Debtors	15
Cash	10
Total	**45**
Current liabilities	
Short-term borrowing	5
Trade creditors	14
Other current liabilities	11
Total	**30**
Current ratio is	**1.5**
(working)	(45/30)
Acid ratio is	**0.83**
(working)	(45 – 20)/30

CALCULATING IT FOR
BP

Figure 13.2 shows how the highlighted numbers from this extract from the accounts of BP combine to produce the "magic number". More information is available at the company's web site at *www.bp.com.* BP is a British-based oil and petrochemical company.

Figure 13.2 Calculating the Current Ratio and Acid Ratio from BP's 1999 Accounts

The figures ...

Summary group balance sheet at 31 December (p. 31 in the published accounts of BP)	**1999** $m	**1998**
Current assets		
Stocks	**5,124**	3,642
Debtors	16,802	12,709
Investments	220	470
Cash at bank and in hand	1,331	405
	23,477	17,226
Creditors – amounts falling due within one year		
Finance debt	**4,900**	4,114
Other creditors	**18,375**	15,329
current assets (liabilities)	202	−2,217

The calculations ...

Current ratio **1.01**
(working) 23,477/(4,900 + 18,375)

BP's current assets total is divided by the total of finance debt and other short-term creditors

Acid ratio **0.79**
(working) (23,477 − 5,124)/(4,900 + 18,375)

BP's current assets minus stocks are divided by the total of finance debt and short-term creditors

These are relatively easy calculations to visualize. The exception is that the BP accounts don't include a total for current liabilities. The "net current assets" figure, shown in the accounts, is the difference between total current assets and the two, separately stated, figures relating to current liabilities ("finance debt" and "other"). These two figures have to be added together to get to total current liabilities. This is the bottom half of the fraction in both ratios.

What it Means

Investors may feel more comfortable with a company that has a liquid balance sheet (plenty of cash and current assets well in excess of current liabilities). But there are plenty of good companies that do not conform to this model. Whether or not a low current ratio and low acid ratio is a cause for concern depends on the nature of the business, the company's own market position, and the saleability or otherwise of its stocks.

BP is a large multinational company producing uniform products that are actively traded around the world. So it need have little concern that it will be unable to sell its stocks, although should the market become aware that it needs to do this, it is so large a factor in the market that the price might be affected.

Another exception to the general rule about liquid balance sheets is in the case of companies that operate in cash businesses and are in a position to dominate their suppliers. A good example here is that of UK supermarket groups. These take cash from customers on a daily basis, but enjoy useful credit terms from suppliers, who they may pay on, say, a monthly basis.

In this instance, the business might have a relatively illiquid "current" balance sheet and a low acid ratio, but nonetheless be perfectly sound. The company's influence in the market allows it to use its suppliers as sources of short-term working capital.

What is good for supermarkets and large multinationals is less good for struggling small companies producing specialized products, which is where these ratios really come into their own.

Magic Number

14

Debtor Days and Creditor Days

The Definition

"Magic number" 13 gave an insight into the way current assets and liabilities are made up. Debtors and creditors are an important part of these items. Debtors (accounts receivable) represent money owed to the company by customers. Creditors (accounts payable) are unpaid bills the company owes to suppliers and others. *Debtor days* and *creditor days* are a way of relating these figures to the company's turnover. They measure how quickly the company is paying its bills, and how much credit it is extending to customers.

The Formulas

Debtor days = Trade debtors × 365/Sales

Creditor days = Trade creditors × 365/Cost of sales

In other words, the ratios are the proportion that year-end trade debtors or creditors represent of annual sales or cost of sales, expressed in days.

The Components

Trade debtors (accounts receivable, or "receivables") – invoiced sales that have not been paid at the balance sheet date. It is important to distinguish between debtors as a whole and trade debtors in particular, although the two figures will sometimes be the same. Trade debtors are used in the calculation.

Trade creditors (accounts payable) – bills for goods and services purchased from suppliers that have not been paid at the balance sheet date. It is important to distinguish between trade creditors and other creditors, such as tax and social security, VAT and other sales, and so on, which typically have fixed payment periods outside the company's control. These are normally excluded from the calculation of creditor days.

Annual sales – "sales", "revenue", and "turnover" are virtually interchangeable terms and are in such common use as to need little further explanation. In the case of calculating debtor days, the sales figure taken should be the one for the year to which the balance sheet debtors and creditors also relate.

Cost of sales – this is the amount subtracted from sales to arrive at gross profit (see "Magic number" 9). The figure comprises the cost of materials: goods and services the company has to buy from outside. This figure is used as part of the calculation of creditor days, because trade creditors represent the proportion of these bills that are unpaid at the year-end. As with the corresponding sales figure, this item should also be the one for the year/year-end to which the creditors relate.

WHERE'S THE DATA?

Trade debtors (accounts receivable or "receivables") – in the notes to the accounts referred to from the current assets' side of the consolidated balance sheet. Occasionally, trade debtors are stated on the face of the balance sheet itself.

Trade creditors (accounts payable) – in the notes to the accounts referred to from the current liabilities ("creditors due within one year") item in the consolidated balance sheet. Occasionally, trade creditors will be stated on the face of the balance sheet.

Annual sales – normally the top-most figure or subtotal in the consolidated profit and loss account or income statement. The total sales figure should be taken.

Cost of sales – this is normally the item immediately below the sales total and above the gross profit figure in the income statement or profit and loss account.

CALCULATING IT – THE THEORY

Figure 14.1 shows the different numbers to be pulled from the accounts and how to use them to calculate the ratio.

Figure 14.1 Calculating the "Magic Number" for ... Debtor Days and Creditor Days

Singapore Widgets Pte has:

Sales of	$100m
Cost of sales of	$80m
Trade debtors of	$25m
Trade creditors of	$18m
Debtor days are	**91 days**
(working)	(25 × 365/100)
Creditor days are	**82 days**
(working)	(18 × 365/80)

CALCULATING IT FOR
McDONALD'S

Figure 14.2 shows how the highlighted numbers from this extract from the accounts of McDonald's combine to produce the "magic numbers".

Figure 14.2 Calculating Debtor Days and Creditor Days from McDonald's 1999 Accounts

The figures ...

Consolidated statement of income (in millions ...) (p. 25 in the published accounts of McDonald's)	**Years ended 31 December**		
	1999	**1998**	**1997**
Sales by company-owned restaurants	9,512.5	8,894.9	8,136.5
Revenues from franchises and affiliates	3,746.8	3,526.5	3,272.3
Total revenue	**13,259.3**	12,421.4	11,408.8
Food and packaging costs and expenses	**3,204.6**	2,997.4	2,772.6

Consolidated balance sheet (in millions ...) (p. 26 in the published accounts of McDonald's)	**At 31 December**	
	1999	**1998**
Current assets		
Cash and equivalents	419.5	299.2
Accounts and notes receivable	**708.1**	609.4
Current liabilities		
Notes payable	1,073.1	686.8
Accounts payable	**585.7**	621.3

The calculations ...

Debtor days **19.5 days**
(working) (708.1 × 365/13,259.3)

McDonald's accounts receivable represent 19.5 days total sales

Creditor days **66.7 days**
(working) (585.7 × 365/3,204.6)

McDonald's typically takes around two months to pay its food and packaging suppliers

The example demonstrates some of the problems involved in calculating these figures. You need to think about the nature of the business to calculate the numbers properly. McDonald's business is a mixture of company-owned restaurants and franchises. The latter pay McDonald's a royalty. Debtor days probably relate partly to sales through owned outlets (largely paid in cash at the time of purchase) and revenue from franchises, probably paid on a monthly basis. This explains why the debtor days figure should be calculated on total revenue, not just company-owned sales.

The creditor days figure is more straightforward. Although cost of sales is not explicitly stated, the only external operating costs appear to relate to food and packaging. With McDonald's operating methods, this makes sense. Hence, the figure throws up that McDonald's pays these outside suppliers on average in 66 days. Extracting such generous credit terms from suppliers is clearly possible because of the company's size and market muscle.

What it Means

Together with stock days (see "Magic number" 15), debtor and creditor days are a crucial link between the company's income statement, its balance sheet, and its cash flow. While in the income statement a company can book sales and profits, if it is slower than before in collecting its bills and suppliers demand faster payment, then cash receipts will not reflect the trend in profits.

As with some other ratios, the absolute level of debtor and creditor days is less important than the trend over time and how the company compares with its competitors.

Different industries collect and pay bills at different speeds, depending on the inherent nature of the business. But if a company's performance in this area is inferior to its competitors (that is, it collects its overdue invoices more slowly and is forced to pay its own debts faster) it is a sign of weakness. Similarly, deterioration in credit control over time is a worrying trend.

As the example of McDonald's shows, some of the best performers in this regard are companies with cash-based businesses and the muscle to negotiate tough terms with their suppliers.

Not all companies are susceptible to this analysis. Creditor days are not meaningful where the company's bought-in cost of sales is low and the company generates most value internally. Asset-based companies and those with long-term contracts may not be suitable cases for analysis. Here, more attention should focus on the length of the company's order book relative to its turnover, and on how revenue from long-term contracts is booked.

Magic Number

15 Stock Days and Stockturn

The Definition

The *stock days* calculation relates the level of a company's stocks to its annual sales and expresses the result as a number of days. This ratio is sometimes called *stockturn*. This is expressed as a multiple: the number of times stock turns over in the course of a year.

The Formulas

Stock days = Stocks × 365/Sales

Stockturn = Sales/Stocks

If expressed in the form of stock days, a lower number of days indicates greater efficiency. If expressed as stockturn, the higher the figure the better, since this indicates faster turnover of stock and hence greater efficiency.

The Components

Stocks (or inventory) – these are stocks of finished goods that have not been sold, or work-in-progress that has not yet been completed. In the case of manufacturing companies, stocks are the result of the company's own production. In the case of retailers, stocks are goods purchased from suppliers but not yet sold.

Annual sales – "sales", "revenue", and "turnover" are virtually interchangeable terms and are in such common use as to need little further explanation. In the case of calculating stock days or stockturn, the sales figure taken should be the one for the year and year-end to which the balance sheet stock figure relates.

WHERE'S THE DATA?

Stocks (or inventory) – this is found in the consolidated (or group) balance sheet in current assets.

Annual sales – this is normally the top-most figure or subtotal in the consolidated profit and loss account or income statement. The total sales figure should be taken.

CALCULATING IT – THE THEORY

Figure 15.1 shows the different numbers to be extracted from the accounts and how to use them to calculate the ratio.

Figure 15.1 Calculating the "Magic Number" for ... Stock Days and Stockturn

Universal Widgets Inc. has:

Annual sales of	$600m
Stocks (or inventory) of	$183m
Stock days are	**111 days**
(working)	(183 × 365/600)

Widget Retail Inc. has:

Annual sales of	$3657m
Stocks (or inventory) of	$457m
Stockturn is	**8 times**
(working)	(3,657/457)

Stockturn and stock days are mirror images of each other

Stockturn can be converted into stock days by dividing it into 365
Similarly, dividing 365 by stock days produces stockturn

CALCULATING IT FOR KINGFISHER

Figure 15.2 shows how the highlighted numbers from this extract from the accounts of the UK-based retail group Kingfisher (see *www.kingfisher.co.uk* for more information) combine to produce the "magic number".

Figure 15.2 Calculating Stock Days and Stockturn from Kingfisher's 2000 Accounts

The figures ...

Consolidated profit and loss account
for the financial year ended 29 January 2000
(p. 45 in the published accounts of Kingfisher)

£m	**2000**	**1999**
Turnover including share of joint ventures		
Continuing operations	10,825.7	6,975.2
Acquisitions	107.4	508.1
less: Share of joint ventures turnover	−48.1	−25.5
	10,885.0	**7,457.8**

Balance sheets
as at 29 January 2000 (p. 47)

	Group	
£m	**2000**	**1999**
Current assets		
Development work in progress	96.7	69.0
Stocks	**1,669.4**	**1,465.4**

The calculations ...

Stock days	**56 days**	**72 days**
(working)	(1,669.4 × 365/10,885.0)	(1,465.4 × 365/7,457.8)

Inventory was held for an average of 56 days before being sold (down from 72 days in the previous year)

Stockturn	**6.5 times**	**5.1 times**
(working)	(10,885.0/1669.4)	(7,457.8/1,465.4)

Kingfisher's inventory was turned over 6.5 times per year in 1999/2000 (up from 5.1 times the previous year)

Although the calculation itself is fairly straightforward, decisions have to be made as to what precisely to include or exclude.

Should you exclude, for example, sales relating to businesses acquired during the year? Strictly speaking, to get a wholly accurate figure, the answer is "yes". However, in practice, it is next to impossible to do this. Stocks attributable to an acquired business cannot be separated from the overall stock figure, and hence taking the global figure is the correct course of action.

In Kingfisher's case there are also joint ventures. In the balance sheet only the share of net assets is included. Stock figures are not given separately. Taking turnover that excludes sales attributable to joint ventures is therefore again, in the absence of any better information, the right course of action.

Finally, the current assets section of the balance sheet includes an item related to "development work in progress". In this instance, the extra information given in the relevant note to the accounts says that it relates to property development projects (that is, new stores) rather than stock. Therefore, it should not be added to the figure for finished stocks.

What it Means

Debtor days, creditor days, and stock days or stockturn are sometimes called working capital ratios. They measure the efficiency with which management is minimizing the amount of day-to-day capital tied up in the form of unsold stocks, uncollected invoices, or unpaid bills.

Once again, as with debtor and creditor days, different industries have different stock cycles. These relate to differences in manufacturing processes or, in the case of retailers like Kingfisher, to the differing types of goods they sell. For obvious reasons, food retailers have faster stockturn (lower stock days) than retailers – like Kingfisher – selling durable goods.

As with debtor and creditor days too, what also matters more is the trend in the ratio rather than its absolute level. Companies in broadly similar businesses should be measured against the ratios achieved by the most efficient company in the industry to see how they stack up.

A problem of interpretation that crops up in the case of Kingfisher is common to all multi-format retailers. A stockturn figure for a retail group operating more than one type of chain – drug stores as well as DIY superstores, for example – may not reveal much about the company's overall efficiency. Slow or declining stockturn in one area may be offset by fast or improving stockturn in another, leaving you none the wiser in pinpointing potential problem areas.

Remember also that stock days (or stockturn) are of no help in assessing a business that does not normally have stocks as part of its day-to-day business – software or intellectual property licensing businesses, bookmakers, and casinos are just some examples of where it is of little use.

Magic Number

16

Gearing

The Definition

Gearing, sometimes called the "debt-equity ratio", is net borrowings divided by tangible shareholders' equity, with the result expressed as a percentage.

The Formula

Gearing = (Total borrowings − cash) × 100/Tangible shareholders' equity

The Components

Total borrowings – this is the sum of all items representing borrowed money or debt securities. It can include both short-term and long-term items. Typically, it takes in bank borrowings and overdrafts, the current portion of long-term debt, medium- and long-term bank borrowings, and currently outstanding bond issues.

Cash – needs little further explanation, except to say that in addition to bank cash it is also sometimes acceptable to add in short-term investments that are near to cash in their characteristics. This means they are easily saleable and not subject to anything other than very small movements in value. Examples of this "near cash" are very short-term government bonds and certificates of deposit.

Shareholders' equity – as indicated in "Magic number" 8, this goes by a number of different names, including "book value", "stockholders (or shareholders' equity)", "shareholders' funds", "net assets" and "net tangible assets". Whatever the terminology, it represents the tangible fixed assets of the business plus current assets, less current liabilities, long-term creditors, and provisions. The difference between these numbers is the residual assets that are "owned" by shareholders.

The alternative way of calculating this figure is to take the total of share capital and reserves and deduct any intangible assets – the value of trademarks or brand names, customer lists, or the goodwill paid when another business is acquired. Goodwill is the amount paid for a business in excess of its asset value. Intangible assets are usually identified separately in the balance sheet.

Where's the Data?

Total borrowings – items that make up this number are located in different parts of the balance sheet. Short-term borrowings are in current liabilities (sometimes called "creditors due within one year"). They are variously identified as bank borrowings, overdrafts, and/or the current portion of long-term debt. Long-term borrowings are normally stated separately, or as part of long-term creditors. You may quite possibly need to add four or five figures together to produce a figure for total borrowings. Borrowings are sometimes assembled in a single note in the accounts, which may simplify their identification and act as a cross-check.

Cash – found in current assets, as a separate and distinct item. It may also be necessary to include some or all of a figure for short-term investments, found in the same place. There is usually some explanation about the nature of the investments, and how they are valued, in the relevant note.

Shareholders' equity – this is found on the face of the consolidated balance sheet, normally using one of the alternative phrases listed earlier. It is also often represented by, and is identifiable as, the total of share capital and various different reserves. As noted previously, intangible assets should be deducted from this figure when calculating gearing.

CALCULATING IT – THE THEORY

Figure 16.1 shows the different numbers to be extracted from the accounts and how to use them to calculate the ratio.

Figure 16.1 Calculating the "Magic Number" for ... Gearing

Tokyo Widgets has the following items in its balance sheet:

	¥bn
Intangible assets	40
Cash	15
Short-term government bonds	5
Bank overdrafts	35
Current portion of long-term debt	25
Long-term borrowings	20
2% Bond 2010	100
Ordinary share capital	20
Capital reserves	200
Revenue reserves	300
Total share capital and reserves	520

Working from the numbers to build up the components of the ratio:

Tangible shareholders' equity is:	480
(working)	(520 − 40)
Cash is	20
(working)	(15 + 5)
Total borrowings are	180
(working)	(35 + 25 + 20 + 100)
Gearing is	**33.30%**
(working)	(180 − 20) × 100/480

CALCULATING IT FOR
SINGAPORE TELECOM

Figure 16.2 shows how the highlighted numbers from this extract from the accounts of SingTel combine to produce the "magic number". SingTel (its web address is *www.singtel.com*) is a Singapore company providing pan-Asian telecommunications and postal services.

Figure 16.2 Calculating Gearing from SingTel's 2000 Accounts

The figures ...

	Group	
Balance sheets as at 31 March (p. 20 in the published accounts of SingTel)	**2000 S$m**	**1999 S$m**
Share capital	2,321.0	2,287.5
Reserves	6,656.9	5,680.4
Share capital and reserves	**8,977.9**	7,967.9
Current assets		
Short-term investments	**1,578.8**	1,475.5
Fixed deposits with financial institutions	**4,162.1**	4,756.6
Cash and bank balances	**168.7**	148.5
Current liabilities		
Bank loans repayable within one year	**0.0**	0.1
Bonds (unsecured)	**100.0**	0.0
Bank overdrafts (unsecured)	**0.1**	0.0
Non-current liabilities		
Bonds (unsecured)	**0.0**	100.0
Deferred taxation	360.0	403.6

The calculation ...

Gearing **−64.70%**

(working) (1,578.8 + 4,162.1 + 168.7 − 100.0 − 0.1) × 100/8,977.9

The three cash items in SingTel's balance sheet less two borrowing items produce a net cash figure, rather than net debt, so the gearing figure is negative

The calculation illustrates one interesting aspect of gearing: it can be employed in reverse when a company has cash and near-cash exceeding its total borrowings. In this case, the ratio tells you that SingTel's net cash represents some 65% of shareholders' equity. This is just as valuable a piece of information as if the figures had been reversed and the company had net borrowings of this percentage.

SingTel is liquid, but this may mean that it has an acquisition in view. Liquid companies may see the income from their cash erode as interest rates fall, just as highly geared companies suffer if interest rates rise.

There is a point of debate about the calculation, which is whether or not one should include SingTel's short-term investments as part of the calculation. The real point here is liquidity.

Further examination of the notes to SingTel's accounts shows that S$221.8 million of the figure under this heading is represented by unquoted investments, while about half of the total is comprised of bonds. To be conservative, any items other than those related to bond investments should be excluded.

What it Means

Gearing provokes more debate than almost any other financial ratio. Like many other "magic numbers", it is the context that is important. Is the gearing ratio significantly higher than that of the company's major competitors? Is the underlying business stable? Does it generate reliable flows of cash? Are the valuations of the company's assets up to date? Are interest rates moving up or down, and how much of the debt is variable rate?

All these factors are important. A high gearing ratio may simply be an indicator that assets are undervalued and therefore that the true shareholders' equity figure is higher than the balance sheet might indicate, and gearing therefore is overstated. Companies with a stable and reliable cash flow can support higher levels of gearing than those in more volatile businesses.

If profits are rising, high gearing can enhance profit growth and returns to equity shareholders. Other things being equal, the profits of highly geared companies can benefit if interest rates are falling and if the debt is paying interest at variable rates.

Equally, assets can be overvalued and gearing therefore understated. High gearing will exaggerate falling profits, and highly geared companies may suffer if interest rates rise.

Financial theory suggests that investors should be indifferent to a company's capital structure, provided that it is minimizing its cost of capital. However, in the real world, gearing does, if nothing else, affect investor sentiment. When times are tough, highly geared companies are seen as vulnerable. They may see their stock market and credit ratings suffer, and find it harder and more costly to borrow.

Magic Number

17 Price/Cash Ratio

The Definition

The *price/cash ratio* compares the market value of a company with its cash and short-term investments. You use this to measure the degree to which liquid assets back up the share price.

The Formulas

Price/Cash ratio = Market capitalization/Cash + Short-term investments

or

Price/Cash ratio = Share price/(Cash + Short-term investments)/ Issued shares outstanding

The Components

Market capitalization – this is the stock market value of the company. You calculate it by multiplying the total of issued shares (or common stock) by their price (see "Magic number" 1). To recap, the components of this calculation are: *issued shares (common stock) outstanding* – shares that have been issued and are publicly listed; and the *share (stock) price* – the current market price of the shares, normally the mid-market price at close of business on the previous trading day.

Cash – this needs little further explanation. In addition to bank cash, it is also sometimes acceptable to include short-term investments that have characteristics similar to cash. This means they will be easily saleable and not subject to anything other than very small movements in value. Examples of "near cash" include very short-term government bonds, certificates of deposit, and the like.

WHERE'S THE DATA?

Issued shares outstanding (in order to calculate market capitalization) – you find these in the notes to the accounts. A reference to the appropriate note will be in the consolidated balance sheet next to the heading "called-up share capital" or a similar term. The number of ordinary shares at the end of the year should be taken, and not their stated nominal money value.

Share (stock) price (in order to calculate market capitalization) – from any daily newspaper or financial web site. Take care to use the actual share price and not that of any options, warrants, partly paid shares, or other derivatives. Financial newspapers also include individual companies' market capitalizations on their share price pages.

Cash – found in current assets, as a separate and distinct item. It may also be necessary to include some or all of a figure for short-term investments, found in the same place.

Calculating it – the Theory

Figure 17.1 shows the different numbers to be extracted from the accounts and how to use them to calculate the ratio.

Figure 17.1 Calculating the "Magic Number" for ... the Price/Cash Ratio

Universal Widgets Inc. has:

Cash of	$50m
Short-term investments of	$25m
Issued shares of	10m
Share price of	$12
Market capitalization is	$120m
(working)	(10 × 12)
Price/cash ratio is	**1.6**
(working)	120/(50 + 25)

Alternatively:

Share price is	$12
Cash per share is	$7.50
(working)	(50 + 25)/10
Price/cash ratio is	**1.6**
(working)	(12/7.50)

CALCULATING IT FOR
SINGAPORE TELECOM

Figure 17.2 shows how the highlighted numbers from this extract from the accounts of SingTel combine to produce the "magic number".

Figure 17.2 Calculating the Price/Cash Ratio from SingTel's 2000 Accounts

The figures ...

	Group	
Balance sheets as at 31 March (p. 20 in the published accounts of SingTel)	**2000 S$m**	**1999 S$m**
Current assets		
Short-term investments	1,578.8	1,475.5
Fixed deposits with financial institutions	4,162.1	4,756.6
Cash and bank balances	168.7	148.5
Current liabilities		
Bank loans repayable within one year	0.0	0.1
Bonds (unsecured)	100.0	0.0
Bank overdrafts (unsecured)	0.1	0.0
Non-current liabilities		
Bonds (unsecured)	0.0	100.0
Deferred taxation	360.0	403.6
Note 2 share capital (p. 25)		
Shares in issue		
Balance as at 31 March (m)	15,473	15,250
Share price at the time of writing	S$2.67	

The calculations ...

Market capitalization	S$41,313m
(working)	(15,473 × 2.67)
Cash and short-term investments	5,809.5
(working)	(1,578.8 + 4,162.1 + 168.7) – (100.0 + 0.1)
Price/cash ratio	**7.1 times**

SingTel's share price is 7.1 times its per-share liquid resources minus debt. The calculation can also be performed by dividing the total of cash and short-term investments by the number of shares, and dividing the result into the share price

The wrinkles in this calculation are close to as described in the previous "magic number". These comprise the question of precisely what to include as part of the cash and liquid resources item. You need to pay precise attention to how short-term investments are stated in the accounts. Particularly important is whether they are included at their cost prices or at some higher, or lower, market value.

Check whether investments are listed or unlisted. Unlisted investments are harder to sell and should not be counted unless it is obvious that their value is substantially in excess of the value included in the balance sheet.

In SingTel's case, a small proportion of the assets fall into this category. For simplicity we have not excluded them from the calculation. In most cases, information on the precise way in which assets have been valued, and on which are listed and which unlisted, is in the relevant notes to the accounts.

What it Means

The price/cash ratio is really only important for companies that have substantial cash in excess of any borrowings.

Companies vary in the ways in which they generate cash and the uses to which they put it. Measuring price to cash over a number of years can demonstrate whether or not the company is generating cash on a regular basis. However, the ratio will be affected by major corporate developments, such as acquisitions or disposals of businesses.

For certain types of company, one important extension of the ratio is to include the balance sheet value of all investments. This applies particularly to institutions, such as banks and insurance companies, which may take deposits or premiums from investors or policyholders, and invest the cash.

In the case of insurance companies, it often happens that investors focus unduly on shorter-term underwriting results (the differences between premiums written and claims made). This ignores the fact that the real value of companies like this lies in the investment portfolios they manage. Because of this myopia, it has sometimes been possible to buy insurance company shares at a substantial discount to the underlying value of their investments.

In the case of more conventional trading companies, one role that this ratio plays is at times when market conditions are difficult. Substantial cash backing for a share can be a considerable source of comfort for investors. It essentially puts a "floor" under the share price, limiting the "downside risk".

Cash per share can be a useful screening mechanism to identify what are sometimes termed "shell" companies.

These are small listed companies with substantial cash resources and few other assets. They are often the subjects of so-called "reverse takeovers". This is where the shell will issue shares to acquire a somewhat larger private company, the shareholders of which then control the combined listed company, gaining access to its cash resources and its listing.

This is often a convenient way for a company to achieve a quick stock market listing and, in some instances, investors in shells can make big profits.

Magic Number

18 Burn Rate

The Definition

The *burn rate* figure is used to work out the number of months before a loss-making company's cash resources run out. You can calculate it by working out monthly operating expenses (or burn rate) from a company's latest reported results, and then dividing this figure into net cash resources. The ratio has recently come into fashion as a way of comparing Internet companies.

The Formula

Months to zero cash = Net cash/Net cash operating expenses per month (that is, burn rate)

The Components

Net cash – this needs little further explanation. In addition to bank cash, it is also sometimes acceptable to include as cash those short-term investments that are near it in their characteristics. These are usually investments that are easily saleable and not subject to anything other than very small movements in value. Examples of this "near cash" are very short-term government bonds, certificates of deposit, and the like.

In the case of cash burn, this distinction must be strictly observed. Less-liquid investments have no place in the calculation. All borrowings should be deducted to arrive at the net cash figure. You can see how to identify borrowings from "Magic number" 16.

Net cash operating expenses ("burn rate") – this is the figure for all operating expenses. It excludes those that are solely book entry items – such as depreciation of fixed assets and amortization of goodwill. These are not counted because they do not represent an actual flow of cash out of the company. Operating expenses normally include those relating to selling and administration, payroll costs, and research and development spending. Any gross profit – the difference between sales and bought-in materials and services – should be deducted from cash operating expenses to arrive at the net figure.

Divide the net cash operating expenses figure by 12 (or six in the case of a half-yearly statement and three in the case of a quarterly statement) to arrive at a per-month figure.

WHERE'S THE DATA?

Net cash – this is found in the group balance sheet in the current assets section, as a separate and distinct item. You can sometimes include some or all of a figure for liquid short-term investments, also found in the same place. Any borrowings should be deducted from the cash figure to arrive at net cash assets.

Net cash operating expenses – you can find gross profit at the top of the profit and loss account or income statement. Gross profit (as explained in "Magic number" 9) is the difference between sales and cost of sales (the cost of bought-in raw materials and services). Cash operating expenses are listed in the notes relating to the income statement. Here, companies are obliged to show the items deducted to arrive at operating profit. Add these up, leaving out any items (such as depreciation, amortization, and provisions) that do not involve a cash movement.

Calculating it – the Theory

Figure 18.2 shows the different numbers to be pulled from the accounts and how to use them to calculate the ratio.

Figure 18.1 Calculating the "Magic Number" for … Burn Rate

The following items are in Universal Widgets' interim balance sheet and income statement:

Six months to December	**£m**
Income statement	
Sales	5.0
Cost of sales	3.0
Gross profit	**2.0**
Operating profit is arrived at after charging:	
Auditors' remuneration	**0.5**
Depreciation	0.7
Amortization of goodwill	0.8
Staff cost	**2.0**
Selling, general and admin. expenses	**4.0**
R&D	**1.0**
Balance sheet as at 31 December	
Cash	15.0
Short-term investments and deposits	2.0
Bank overdraft	1.5
Long-term borrowings	0.5
Net cash operating expenses	5.5
(working)	(1 + 4 + 2 + 0.5 − 2)
Net cash operating expenses per month (burn rate)	0.916
(working)	(5.5/6 months)
Net cash resources	15.0
(working)	(15 + 2 − 1.5 − 0.5)
Months to zero cash	**16.4 months**
(working)	(15.0/0.916)

CALCULATING IT FOR
INTERACTIVE INVESTOR INTERNATIONAL

Figure 18.2 shows how the highlighted numbers from this extract from the accounts of Interactive Investor International combine to produce the "magic number". Interactive Investor International (*www.iii.co.uk*) is a personal finance and investment portal site.

Figure 18.2 Calculating Burn Rate from Interactive Investor International Interim 2000 Report

The figures ...

Consolidated income statement for second quarter and six months ended 31 March 2000
(p. 10 in the published accounts of Interactive Investor International)

(£000s)		**2000**
Net revenues		2,751
Cost of revenues		2,031
Gross profit		**720**
Operating expenses		**11,022**
of which:	Depreciation	**312**
	Compensation in shares	**467**
	Deferred compensation	**2,307**

Consolidated balance sheet at 31 March 2000 (p. 11)

Cash at bank and in hand	**72,770**
Creditors and provisions	**9,839**

The calculations ...

Net cash operating expenses	7,216
(working)	(11,022 − 312 − 467 − 2,307 − 720)
Net cash operating expenses per month (burn rate)	1,203
(working)	(7,216/6)
Cash less short-term creditors	62,931
(working)	(72,770 − 9,839)
Months to zero cash	**52 months**
(working)	(62,931/1,203)

On their present rate of spending, Interactive's cash will take over four years to run out

Figure 18.2 shows some of the problems encountered when calculating this ratio. It is essential that the most up-to-date figures be used. If these are from interim or quarterly statements, sufficient detail may not be present to allow the calculation to be performed with absolute certainty.

In the case of Interactive Investor International, there is no explicit analysis of operating expenses, although depreciation and other non-cash items can be extracted from the notes reconciling the cash flow statement to the income statement.

Similarly, there is no analysis of short-term creditors. Normally, this would allow you to work out what portion of this figure is short-term debt. In the absence of other information it is best to subtract all short-term creditors to arrive at the figure for available cash resources.

What it Means

Companies cannot make losses forever. Eventually they run out of money. Burn rate shows how much time loss-making businesses have before they need to be making sufficient profits to cover their expenses, or else will require further fundraising to be able to pay their bills.

Calculating burn rates on a half-year by half-year basis shows how well companies are progressing at generating profits, or reducing losses and controlling their expenses. The unpredictable part of this is the receptiveness or otherwise of the market to further attempts at fundraising. Companies caught between a high burn rate, dwindling cash, and an unreceptive market face oblivion and are best avoided.

Magic Number

19 Return on Capital Employed

The Definition

Return on capital employed (ROCE) is one of several ratios that compare profits made to assets used in the business. Return on capital is the percentage that profit before interest and tax (PBIT) represents of net capital employed (NCE).

Net capital employed is the capital provided for use in the business by equity shareholders, and other long-term creditors and providers of capital such as bondholders.

ROCE is often calculated as the average of opening and closing capital employed. You do this because it is the capital employed during the year (not at the year-end) that generates the return. If calculated this way, the ratio is called "return on average capital employed" (ROACE).

The Formulas

ROCE = Profit before interest and tax × 100/Net capital employed

ROACE = Profit before interest and tax × 100/
(Net capital employed at prior year-end
+ Net capital employed at latest year-end)/2

The Components

Net capital employed (NCE) – this is the capital provided for use in the business by equity shareholders and other long-term creditors and providers of capital such as bondholders. You can work it out quite simply by taking the total of all balance sheet assets and deducting current liabilities. Current liabilities are excluded because they are not permanently available capital.

Average capital employed – this is the capital employed at the beginning of the year (in effect, the capital employed figure for the prior year-end) plus the net capital employed at the end of the year, with the total divided by two to produce the average.

Profit before interest and tax (PBIT) – this is calculated simply by adding back the interest charge to the pre-tax profit figure.

WHERE'S THE DATA?

Net capital employed – this is often given as a separate item in the consolidated or group balance sheet, usually about half way down the page. If the figure is not given, total assets should be clearly visible and current liabilities (creditors due within one year) should be deducted from total assets to arrive at net capital employed. Most accounts contain at least two years' data, so you can calculate opening capital employed by using the same data for the prior year.

Profit before interest and tax – this is found in the income statement or profit and loss account. Pre-tax profit and the interest charge can usually be easily identified without recourse to the notes. Remember, however, that if the company has net interest earned rather than net interest paid (that is, if the company has net cash rather than net borrowings), PBIT will be less than the pre-tax profit figure.

Calculating it – the Theory

Figure 19.1 shows the different numbers to be pulled from the accounts and how to use them to calculate the ratio.

Figure 19.1 Calculating the "Magic Number" for ... Return on Capital

Aussie Widgets Pty Ltd has relevant profit and loss and balance sheet numbers as follows:

	2000	**1999**
	A$m	**A$m**
Operating profit	20	18
Associated companies	5	4
less: Interest paid	3	3
Pre-tax profit	22	19
Intangible assets	15	15
Fixed assets	150	145
Current assets	25	20
Total assets	190	180
Creditors – due within one year	30	26
Pre-interest profit is	25	22
(working)	(22 + 3)	(19 + 3)
Net capital employed is	160	154
(working)	(190 – 30)	(180 – 26)
Average capital employed is	157	
(working)	(160 + 154)/2	
Return on capital employed is	**15.6%**	
(working)	(25 × 100)/160	
Return on average capital employed is	**15.9%**	
(working)	(25 × 100)/157	

Note that average capital employed for 1999 cannot be calculated without the year-end 1998 figures

CALCULATING IT FOR

NTT

Figure 19.2 shows how the highlighted numbers from this extract from the accounts of NTT combine to produce the "magic number".

Figure 19.2 Calculating Return on Capital from NTT's 2000 Accounts

The figures ...

		As at 31 March
Consolidated balance sheet	**2000**	**1999**
(subtotals from accounts in billions of yen)		
(p. 38 in the published accounts of NTT)		
Current assets	**3,918**	**3,697**
Property, plant, and equipment	**12,162**	**11,864**
Investments and other assets	**2,494**	**3,541**
Current liabilities	**3,744**	**3,858**

Consolidated statement of income year ended 31 March (rounded to billions of yen) (p. 40)	**2000**	**1999**
Operating income	872	711
Other expenses		
Interest etc.	**235**	216
Interest income	**−2**	−7
Gains on sales of stock	0	−1,634
Other	−17	23
Total other expenses	217	−1,403
Income before income taxes	**656**	2,114

The calculations ...

	2000	1999
Net capital employed	14,830	15,244
(working)	(3,918 + 12,162 + 2,494 − 3,744)	(3,697 + 11,864 + 3,541 − 3,858)
Average capital employed	15,037	
(working)	(14,830 + 15,244)/2	
PBIT	889	
(working)	(656 + 235 − 2)	
Return on capital	**5.99%**	
(working)	(889 × 100)/14,830	

NTT's PBIT is divided by the capital employed figure for 2000 and expressed as a percentage.

Return on average capital	**5.91%**
(working)	(889 × 100)/15037

NTT's PBIT is divided by the average capital employed for the two years and expressed as a percentage

The figures show some of the difficulties in arriving at an accurate calculation. In the case of the 2000 figures, working out the profit before interest and tax item is straightforward. The prior year, however, contained a large exceptional item that could wholly distort the calculation. In cases like this, you need to use judgment in deciding which is the normal ongoing level of profit before tax before adding back interest paid to get to PBIT.

The other point arising from the example is that NTT's capital employed fell during the period in question. This means that return on average capital was a lower figure than return on year-end capital, the reverse of normal. NTT's return on capital is also very low in absolute terms.

What it Means

It is easy to become confused by different return figures, and the differences between them can be given an importance that is not warranted. Good companies have a high return on capital; bad ones often have a low one. But even this distinction is not absolute. Cyclical stocks can show sharply fluctuating levels of profitability. Buy them at the right point in the cycle and they will be profitable investments, even though their returns may look low.

Return on capital does not distinguish between the different types of capital on which the return is earned; it simply measures the return generated by the company on the capital, irrespective of its source or cost.

Measuring ROCE against cost of capital can be revealing. But in this case you need to work out the return using an after-tax version of PBIT. This is usually called NOPLAT (net operating profits less adjusted taxes). Tax is subtracted from conventional PBIT, but an adjustment is made to take account of the fact that adding back interest means that some extra notional tax should be added into the equation. You calculate the return in the normal way. How to work out cost of capital is covered in "Magic number" 29.

The reason that companies perform poorly against their peers is usually down to inefficient management of assets – too many under-performing peripheral businesses – or else to factors outside the company's control, perhaps a tough regulatory regime.

In NTT's case, its ROCE of around 6% compares with a similar figure in the same year for British Telecom, for example, of 16%, BT hardly being known as a paragon of efficiency.

The figures really need to be set against the companies' respective cost of capital to make a definitive comparison. Unless a company makes a return over and above its cost of capital, it is in effect gradually destroying the capital base of the business. Shareholders are the ultimate victims of this process. This makes ROCE a vital measuring gauge.

Magic Number

20 Return on Average Equity

The Definition

Return on equity (ROE) is another ratio connecting the income statement to the balance sheet. It compares profits attributable to equity shareholders with assets owned by shareholders. Net profits after all deductions (with the exception of equity shareholders' dividends) are expressed as a percentage of shareholders' equity.

As with return on capital employed, the ratio is often calculated on the *average* of opening and closing shareholders' equity (ROAE). Shareholders' equity should include intangibles and goodwill, especially any previously accumulated goodwill not reflected in the balance sheet.

The Formulas

ROE = Net profit attributable to shareholders × 100/Shareholders' equity

ROAE = Net profit attributable × 100/(Equity at prior year-end + Equity at latest year-end)/2

The Components

Net profit attributable – this is defined as profits after all deductions, with the exception of ordinary share dividends. The idea is to get to profits that are solely attributable to (or "owned" by) ordinary shareholders. Profits should therefore be taken after all tax, minority interests, and preference share dividends (if any).

Shareholders' equity – this goes by a number of different names. They include "stockholders' (or shareholders') equity", "shareholders' funds", and "net assets". In most instances, take the figure that represents the fixed assets of the business plus current assets. Then subtract current liabilities, long-term creditors, and provisions. The difference between these numbers represents the residual assets that are "owned" by shareholders.

In contrast to the calculation used for book value in "Magic number" 8, for the purposes of calculating return on equity, all intangible assets should be included. This is particularly true of any accumulated goodwill that is not recognized on the face of the balance sheet, irrespective of whether it has been written off. If necessary, this should be added back to enlarge shareholders' equity.

This is a very important distinction. Return on equity is one of the crucial tests of management effectiveness. So it is important to include in the denominator all of the capital that has been spent by management, not just what it has chosen to recognize on the face of the balance sheet. The cumulative goodwill item may change from year to year and should therefore be identified separately for each year if you are calculating return on average equity.

Where's the Data?

Net profit attributable – this is stated on the face of the profit and loss account toward the bottom of the page. The figure should be taken after deducting preference dividends and minority interests (if any).

Shareholders' equity – this is given in the consolidated balance sheet, normally labeled with one of the alternative phrases listed earlier. It is also identifiable as the total of share capital and various different reserves. Take care, however, to determine whether or not it includes any intangible assets. Cumulative goodwill written off is normally located in the notes to the accounts, usually (in the case of UK companies) in the note relating to shareholders' funds or fixed assets.

CALCULATING IT – THE THEORY

Figure 20.1 shows the different numbers to be pulled from the accounts and how to use them to calculate the ratio.

Figure 20.1 Calculating the "Magic Number" for ... Return on Average Equity

Universal Widgets plc has the following profit and loss and balance sheet numbers:

Year to December	**2000**	**1999**
Profit before tax	50	40
less: Taxation	15	12
Profit after tax	35	28
less: Minority interests	1	1
Attributable profit	34	27
Share capital	15	15
Revenue reserve	50	44
Capital reserves	100	100
Total share capital and reserves	165	159
Cumulative goodwill written off prior to 1 January 1998	20	20
Adjusted shareholders' equity	185	179
(working)	(165 + 20)	(159 + 20)
Average adjusted shareholders' equity	182	
(working)	(185 + 179)/2	
Return on adjusted average equity is	**18.68%**	
(working)	(34 × 100)/182	

This example shows the difference that the goodwill element in the calculation can make. If the ratio were to be calculated on the latest figure for shareholders' equity excluding goodwill, the return on equity would be 20.6% (34 × 100 divided by 165), almost two percentage points higher than the preferred method of calculating it, so overstating management's efforts. Thinking of cumulative goodwill as extra cash spent on past acquisitions makes it easier to see why it should be included.

CALCULATING IT FOR KINGFISHER

Figure 20.2 shows how the highlighted numbers from this extract from the accounts of Kingfisher combine to produce the "magic number".

Figure 20.2 Calculating Return on Average Equity from Kingfisher's 2000 Accounts

The figures ...

Consolidated profit and loss account for the financial year ended 29 January (p. 45 in the published accounts of Kingfisher) **£ millions**	**2000**	**1999**
Profit on ordinary activities before taxation	726.2	629.3
Tax on profit on ordinary activities	−204.4	−183.5
Profit on ordinary activities after taxation	521.8	445.8
Equity minority interests	−102.4	−8.9
Profit for the financial year attributable to the members of Kingfisher	419.4	436.9
Dividends on equity shares	−198.2	−175.3
Retained profit for the financial year	221.2	261.6

Balance sheet as at 29 January (p. 47)	2000	1999
Capital and reserves		
Called-up share capital	171	170
Share premium account	255.2	237.7
Revaluation reserve	534.4	395.4
Non-distributable reserves	148.2	146.3
Profit and loss account	1,519.8	1,301.2
Equity shareholders' funds	2,628.6	2,250.6
Equity minority interests	456.9	365.7
	3,085.5	2,616.3

Note 31 Reserves (p. 69)

The cumulative amount of goodwill written off directly to reserves at the start and end of the year in respect of undertakings still within the group is **£1,541.2 million**

The calculations ...

Year-end adjusted shareholders' equity	4,169.8	3,791.8
(working)	(1,541.2 + 2,628.6)	(1,541.2 + 2,250.6)

Average adjusted shareholders' equity	3,980.8
	(4,169.8+3,791.8)/2
Return on average equity	**10.54%**
(working)	(419.4 × 100/3,980.8)

Kingfisher's after-tax profits are expressed as a percentage of its shareholders' equity adjusted for goodwill previously written off. If unadjusted shareholders' equity were used, the ROAE, on the year-end figure, would be 15.96%. This is profits of £419.4 million as a percentage of equity of £2,628.6 million.

The calculation illustrates the importance of taking into account any goodwill figures that have been directly written off to reserves. In this case, the difference is a number (about 16%) that appears half reasonable and one (around 10%) that looks considerably less impressive. Elsewhere in the balance sheet, Kingfisher does disclose goodwill of £397.4 million, which is automatically included as part of shareholders' funds.

The rather larger figure includes other goodwill that has been generated by past acquisitions and had been written off. Nonetheless, it should still be used in the calculation. It represents what management has paid out in the past for acquisitions over and above their tangible assets. You need to include this to see how financially productive these acquisitions have been.

Accounting policies have changed recently in the UK to make companies include purchased goodwill of this sort in their accounts for new acquisitions, but goodwill figures hidden in the notes will be a feature for some time to come. Other countries treat goodwill in different ways. The important point is always to make sure that all goodwill found both on and off the balance sheet is included.

What it Means

ROAE is vital for appraising companies correctly. It is easy to see that the higher the figure, the more value should be created for shareholders. The return can either be distributed in dividends or retained within the company. Provided management can produce consistent returns, the higher the proportion retained, the more future growth is underpinned. "Magic number" 31 covers this point in much more detail.

Companies with high returns on equity typically include the classic "people businesses" and companies adding a high element of value to bought-in material. Good examples include software companies and consultancy firms.

Low-return businesses are best avoided unless there are special reasons for doing so (for example, heavily undervalued assets or the possibility of strong recovery), or unless they appear exceptionally cheap. Companies in the same sector should have a similar ROAE. Compare the best with the rest.

Magic Number

21 Net Tangible Asset Value

The Definition

Net tangible asset value (usually shortened to NTA or NAV) is calculated by taking shareholders' funds and, after excluding any goodwill, expressing the result on a per-share basis. You do this by dividing the absolute amount by the number of shares in issue at the year-end. It is typically used for asset-based businesses, such as property companies or investment trusts.

The Formula

NTA = Equity shareholders' funds – Goodwill (if any)/Year-end shares in issue

The Components

Net tangible assets – as indicated earlier, NTA goes by a number of different names, including "stockholders' (or shareholders') equity", "shareholders' funds", "net assets", "book value", and so on. Whatever term is used, it represents the tangible fixed assets of the business plus current assets, less current liabilities, long-term creditors, and provisions. The difference between these numbers represents the residual assets that are "owned" by shareholders. Often balance sheets will include some element of goodwill or intangible assets. In contrast to the previous "magic number", in this instance goodwill is excluded from NTA.

Issued shares (common stock) outstanding – shares that have been issued and are publicly listed.

The shares outstanding at the balance sheet date should be used for the calculation, but adjusted for any subsequent stock splits. If there have been shares issued since the year-end, any money raised or tangible assets acquired as a result should also be included.

Where's the Data?

Net tangible assets – these are on the face of the consolidated balance sheet, and are normally found by looking for one of the terms listed earlier. NTA is also, in effect, the total of share capital and various different reserves. However, balance sheet goodwill or intangible assets should be deducted. This item is normally found toward the top of the page, close to fixed assets.

Issued shares (common stock) outstanding – these are in the notes to the accounts. The note can be found from a reference in the consolidated balance sheet adjoining the heading "called-up share capital" or a similar term. The number of ordinary shares at the end of the year should be taken, and not their stated nominal money value (if any).

The number of shares used to calculate earnings per share should not be used. This will normally be an average for the year, not the most recent figure. In this instance, the most recent figure is the one to use.

Calculating it – the Theory

Figure 21.1 shows the different numbers to be pulled from the accounts and how to use them to calculate the ratio.

Figure 21.1 Calculating the "Magic Number" for ... Net Tangible Asset Value

Widget Investments Inc. has balance sheet information as follows:

Shareholders' funds are	$200m
The investment portfolio valued at the lower of cost or market value is	$180m
Intangible assets are	$5m
Unrealised capital gains (net of tax) are	$120m
Issued shares at the year-end are	25m
Net tangible assets are	$195m
(working)	(200 – 5)
Net tangible assets including capital gains are	$315m
(working)	(195 + 120)
Net tangible assets per share are	**$7.80**
(working)	(195/25)
Net tangible assets per share including gains are	**$12.60**
(working)	(315/25)

CALCULATING IT FOR

GREAT UNIVERSAL STORES

Figure 21.2 shows how the highlighted numbers from this extract from the accounts of GUS combine to produce the "magic number".

Figure 21.2 Calculating Net Tangible Assets from Great Universal Stores' 2000 Accounts

The figures ...

Group balance sheet at 31 March (p. 44 in the published accounts of GUS)	**2000** **£m**	**1999** **£m**
Fixed assets		
Goodwill	**1,437.6**	**1,503.5**
Other intangible assets	**139.1**	**123.4**
Other investments at cost	**15.0**	**8.4**
Total share capital and reserves	**2,466.3**	**2,397.0**
Market value of investments	**108.8**	**8.4**
Net assets Burberry (p. 20) (from divisional trading report)	97.0	85.0

Note 25 (p. 60)

At 31 March, **1,005,888,345 (1999 – 1,005, 769,504)** shares had been allotted called up and fully paid

The calculations ...

	2000	1999
Net tangible assets are	889.6	770.1
(working)	(2,466.3 − 1,437.6 − 139.1)	(2,397 − 1,503.5 − 123.4)

This is the shareholders' equity figure less goodwill and other intangible assets

	2000	1999
Net tangible assets with investments at market value are	983.4	770.1
(working)	(889.6 − 15 + 108.8)	(770.1 − 8.4 + 8.4)

This is the net tangible assets figure calculated above, but substituting market value of investments for their value at cost

	2000	1999
Net tangible assets per share (pence)	**88.4**	**76.6**
(working)	(889.6/1,005.9)	(770.1/1,005.8)
NTA per share (with invs. at market value)	**97.8**	**76.6**
(working)	(983.4/1,005.9)	(as above)

Figures calculated earlier are divided by the respective shares issued (in millions) to arrive at the per-share NTA figures

The example of GUS shows some of the limitations of the calculation, but also the way in which it can be tailored for later events.

Much of the goodwill in the GUS balance sheet relates to the recent takeover of the Argos catalogue showroom business. This is a well-established retailing format in the UK.

The value of the calculation as it stands is limited, because GUS is known within the UK to be an asset-rich company that has habitually understated the real value of its assets. Scrutinizing the notes to the accounts and recent press comment throws up one or two clues. For example, GUS revalues its trading properties only very infrequently. The last such valuation, according to the accounts, was in 1996. Consequently, the assets in question are likely to be substantially undervalued.

Second, GUS owns the Burberry retail chain. It has plans for a partial initial public offering (IPO) of this business in 2001 or 2002. The mooted price for the sale is in the region of £2 billion. The value of Burberry's net assets in the GUS balance sheet is £97 million.

Hence, the flotation of Burberry could produce a substantial addition to net tangible assets. Burberry also has a number of prime high street sites in central London and other parts of the world that may or may not be included as part of the IPO.

What it Means

Although seemingly a simple calculation, calculating NTA can involve major detective work. Make sure to comb the notes to the accounts for any relevant information. Try and identify any differences between the market value of assets and their value as stated in the balance sheet, and take note of the valuation dates of assets such as property. If IPOs are mooted for a part of the business, compare its net assets with the expected value of the business when floated.

It is often the case that there will be substantial differences between the way different companies value assets. This is true both within the same country and between similar companies in different countries.

These differences can be a source of substantial share price appreciation. All that is needed is a reasonable chance that the market will recognize the anomaly at some future date, either via a takeover or through break-ups and spin-offs.

Changes of management can often be a catalyst for changes in strategy to unlock value. Companies with controlling shareholdings in the hands of a family or individual are less susceptible to market pressure to unlock value.

In the case of GUS, for example, the changes started when the Wolfson family released its earlier tight control over the group by dismantling the two-tier voting structure in the shares. Outside management has since been recruited.

Magic Number

22 Premium/(Discount) to NAV

The Definition

The *premium/discount to NAV* is the percentage difference between the share (stock) price and the per-share net asset value of the company. If the share price is less than the per-share NAV, it is said to be "at a discount"; if more than the NAV per share, it is said to be "at a premium". Net asset value is similar in concept to book value or net tangible assets. Premium or discount to NAV is frequently used for evaluating asset-based companies, such as property companies and investment trusts.

The Formula

Premium or (discount) = (Share price × 100/Net asset value) − 100

If the resulting figure is negative, the number is the percentage discount; if positive, it is the percentage premium.

The Components

Net asset value – use the definition for net tangible assets in the previous section, but adjust the figure to ensure that calculations take account of the current market value of any properties and investments.

To recap, net tangible assets, or NTA, goes by a number of different names, including "stockholders' (or shareholders') equity", "shareholders' funds", "net assets", and "book value". Take the tangible fixed assets of the business plus current assets, and subtract current liabilities, long-term creditors, and provisions. The resulting number represents the residual assets that are "owned" by shareholders. Exclude any goodwill stated on the face of the balance sheet, and substitute market value for book value of investments if necessary.

Issued shares (common stock) outstanding – these are shares that have been issued and are publicly listed.

The shares outstanding at the point in time the calculation is performed should be used for the calculation. Normally, this is the year-end figure obtained from the annual report but adjusted for any subsequent stock splits.

Share (stock) price – the current market price of the shares, normally the mid-market price at close of business on the previous trading day.

Where's the Data?

Net asset value – this is on the face of the consolidated balance sheet. It may be identified by one of the alternative phrases listed earlier. For additional information, look also in the notes to the accounts relating to fixed assets (especially property) and investments, especially investments in marketable securities. Balance sheet goodwill or intangible assets should be deducted. These are normally found at the top of the page, close to fixed assets.

Issued shares (common stock) outstanding – these are in the notes to the accounts. The note can be found from the reference in the consolidated balance sheet next to the heading "called-up share capital". The number of ordinary shares at the end of the year should be taken, and not their stated nominal money value (if any).

The number of shares used to calculate earnings per share should not be used. This will normally be an average for the year, not the most recent figure. Use the most recent year-end figure.

Share (stock) price – from any daily newspaper or financial web site. Take note of the units in which the share price is expressed. In the UK, shares are traditionally quoted in pence, so NAV calculations must be reduced to the same unit.

Calculating it – the Theory

Figure 22.1 shows the different numbers to be pulled from the accounts and how to use them to calculate the ratio.

Figure 22.1 Calculating the "Magic Number" for ... Premium/(Discount) to NAV

As in Figure 21.1, Widget Investments Inc. has balance sheet information as follows:

Shareholders' funds are	$200m
The investment portfolio valued at the lower of cost or market value is	$180m
Intangible assets are	$5m
Unrealised capital gains (net of tax) are	$120m
Issued shares at the year-end are	25m
The current share price is	$10
Net tangible assets are	$195m
(working)	(200 − 5)
NAV (net tangible assets including capital gains) is	$315m
(working)	(195 + 120)
NAV per share is	$12.60
(working)	(315/25)
Discount to NAV is	**20.60%**
(working)	(10 × 100)/12.6) − 100 (= 79.4 − 100.0, or − 20.6)

CALCULATING IT FOR

GREAT UNIVERSAL STORES

Figure 22.2 shows how the highlighted numbers from this extract of GUS's accounts – also shown in part in the previous section – combine to produce the "magic number".

Figure 22.2 Calculating Premium/(Discount) to NAV from Great Universal Stores' 2000 Accounts

The figures ...

Group balance sheet at 31 March (p. 44 in the published accounts of GUS)	**2000** **£m**	**1999** **£m**
Fixed assets		
Goodwill	**1,437.6**	**1,503.5**
Other intangible assets	**139.1**	**123.4**
Other investments at cost	**15.0**	**8.4**
Total share capital and reserves	**2,466.3**	**2,397.0**
Market value of investments	**108.8**	**8.4**
Net assets Burberry (p. 20) (from divisional trading report)	97.0	85.0

Note 25 (p. 60)

At 31 March, **1,005,888,345 (1,999 – 1,005, 769,504)** shares had been allotted called up and fully paid

GUS's share price at the time of writing	**523p**	

The calculations ...

Net tangible assets	889.6	770.1
(working)	(2,466.3 – 1,437.6 – 139.1)	(2,397 – 1,503.5 – 123.4)

This is the shareholders' equity figure less goodwill and other intangible assets

Net tangible assets with investments at market value	983.4	770.1
(working)	(889.6 – 15 + 108.8)	(770.1 – 8.4 + 8.4)

The net tangible assets figure is as calculated above, but substituting market value of investments for their value at cost

NTA per share (with investment at market value)	97.8	76.6
(working)	(983.4/1,005.9)	(770.1 /1,005.8)

Figures calculated earlier are divided by the respective shares issued (in millions) to arrive at the per-share NTA figures

Premium to NAV	**435%**	**582%**
	(523 × 100/97.8) − 100	(523 × 100/76.6) − 100

From the previous section we deduced that the IPO of Burberry might increase GUS's NAV by 189p per share

Adding this to the NAV prices of 97.8p calculated above would reduce the premium to NAV represented by the current share price to 82%. NAV including Burberry is approximately 98 + 189p or 287p

The percentage change required to get from 287p to the current share price of 523p is 82%

We commented in the previous section on the nature of the calculation. Calculating premium or discount to NAV merely takes the process a stage further, taking one of the calculations performed last time (tangible net assets, adjusted to reflect investments at market value) and comparing it with the current share price. Including the Burberry note is legitimate because the IPO has been announced, and should result in GUS being able to "mark to market" its investment in Burberry, much as it does with other investments.

WHAT IT MEANS

Ostensibly, even including Burberry, GUS does not appear "cheap" by this measure. But this only highlights that the company is in a phase of transition from being a recognized "asset play" to one where the share price is more driven by profits.

Premium or discount to NAV is more frequently used as a yardstick for property investment companies and investment trusts. Here, properties or investments are regularly revalued. There is less guesswork needed in calculating the true NAV.

As with earnings growth and price-earnings ratios, whether the shares stand on a premium or discount to NAV depends on how successful or otherwise management is at generating consistent growth in assets.

The more successful, the greater is the chance that investors will be prepared to pay a premium to asset value. The duller its performance, the more likely it is that the shares will stand on a significant discount. Property investment companies and investment trusts, while not entirely homogeneous, are sufficiently similar to make this ratio widely used as a way of comparing them with their peers in the same category, both within a single national market and internationally.

Part Four

Cash Flow–Based "Magic Numbers"

CASH FLOW-BASED "MAGIC NUMBERS"

Cash, as they say, is king. And what is important about the "magic numbers" based around a company's cash flow statements is that, unlike profits, they cannot be fudged, smoothed, or manipulated.

If in doubt, look to the cash flow statement to find out what really happened. Were a company's profits artificially high because of changes in depreciation policy? Were they inflated because the company was producing for stock? Or was the company having to pay its bills faster or grant customers more favorable credit terms?

The "magic numbers" in this part are few and relatively easy to work out, but they are crucial for evaluating a company.

- Free cash flow is the basis for several other key measures and can be calculated fairly accurately and simply. It shows you how much a company has generated after all essential bills have been paid (especially interest and tax).
- Spending on fixed assets as a multiple of depreciation is important. Companies usually spend more than they have set aside to replace worn-out assets. The more a company is growing, the bigger the extra amount. But if a company is producing a poor return on its capital, this spending could be futile.
- Compare operating cash flow with operating profits and you get a view of how efficiently a company's profits translate into cash. Most companies should have operating cash flow in excess of their operating profits.
- Finally, price to free cash flow is the cash flow statement's counterpart to the price-earnings ratio. It uses free cash flow, rather than earnings, as the number that is divided into the price. It needs careful interpretation, but is a more reliable (if less well-used) indicator.

Not all of these numbers are applicable to every company, although price to cash flow and operating cash flow to operating profit tend to work well for most. Only the ratio relating to depreciation is less generally used. This is because certain types of company may not have a particularly heavy requirement for fixed assets in order to run their businesses efficiently.

Equally important, free cash flow has an absolutely vital role when it comes to valuing companies using discounted cash flow (see "Magic number" 30 in Part Five).

The pivotal role that cash and cash flow-related numbers play in assessing whether or not a company is sound explains why some companies are reluctant to display too much detail. In many countries, cash flow statements are an afterthought. It is common not to give cash flow numbers at the half-way stage of the year.

Cash flow is (supposedly) a more difficult concept to grasp and analysts are by nature lazy. The result is that these ratios are not used as often as they should be by both professional investors and private investors alike. So you can get a real edge in stock selection if you persevere with them.

Magic Number

23

Free Cash Flow

The Definition

Cash flow is different to profits. It ignores book-entry transactions and concentrates purely on the flows of cash into and out of a business. Hence, operating cash flow (the cash flow counterpart to operating profit) ignores depreciation, amortization of goodwill, retained profits of minority-owned companies, capitalized interest, and any other concepts that are merely the result of accounting conventions. *Free cash flow* (FCF) goes further. In addition, it subtracts those items that a company cannot avoid paying if it wants to stay in business: interest, tax, and sufficient capital spending to maintain its fixed assets.

The Formula

FCF = Operating cash flow − Interest − Tax − Maintenance capital spending

The Components

Operating cash flow – sometimes called "net cash from operating activities" or "net cash inflow from operating activities", this figure is the result of adjusting operating profit for items that affect the way profit is calculated but do not represent movements of cash. These items include depreciation and amortization, provisions, retained profits of associated or related (partly-owned) companies, and changes in debtors, creditors, and stocks. Most companies show how operating cash flow is arrived at in detail.

Interest paid – this is cash interest paid in the year in question. It may not coincide exactly with the amount stated in the profit and loss account, depending on the timing of interest payments and whether or not any interest is capitalized. Interest must be paid in full on the due date. Whether or not a company capitalizes interest (that is, ignores it in the income statement) does not alter the reality that capitalized interest still represents a cash cost to the business.

Tax paid – this is the tax paid in cash in the year in question. This may not be the figure the company provides for in the income statement for the year in question. For example, taxes on profits of one year may be paid in the next.

Maintenance capital spending – this is the capital spending on fixed assets required to maintain the business's assets in good order, replacing those that are worn out. In the absence of any guidance from management in the report, it may be necessary to guess this figure, perhaps assuming it will be roughly two-thirds of the total figure for capital spending.

Where's the Data?

Operating cash flow – this is in the cash flow statement toward the top of the page. Avoid confusing the figure for operating cash flow with that of operating profit. Cash flow tables often start with operating profit as the top-most figure and then show how the various adjustments combine to produce operating cash flow. In other cases, the reconciliation of the two figures is contained in a note.

Interest paid – this is in the section of the cash flow statement labeled "net cash inflow or outflow from servicing of finance or financial investment", or some combination of these words. Net interest (that is, interest paid less interest received) should be taken, together with any items that amount to interest (leasing instalments and regular debt repayments, for example). Large one-off items should be ignored.

Tax paid – this is given in a separate section of the tax flow statement, usually a single-line item.

Maintenance capital spending – this is in the cash flow statement or the notes relating to it, under the heading "net cash outflow for capital expenditure, purchase of fixed assets, and financial investment" – or some combination of these words. Payments for acquisitions (usually termed "purchase of subsidiaries" and the like), and any suspiciously large one-off items, can be ignored.

Calculating it – the Theory

Figure 23.1 shows the different numbers to be pulled from the accounts and how to use them to calculate the ratio.

Figure 23.1 Calculating the "Magic Number" for ... Free Cash Flow

Tokyo Widgets has the following items in its cash flow statement:

	¥m
Net cash inflow from operations	100
Depreciation	20
Amortization of goodwill	25
Interest paid	−15
Tax paid	−22
Purchases of fixed assets	−17
Sales of fixed assets	2
Free cash flow before capital is spent	63
(working)	(100 − 15 − 22)

Note that depreciation and amortization are not deducted as they have already been accounted for in arriving at net cash inflow from operations

Maintenance capital spending	−10
(working)	two-thirds (say) of −17 + 2)
Free cash flow is	**53**

Note also the convention in the cash flow statement that outflows have a minus sign and inflows a plus sign

Non-cash items are positive if they represent P&L deductions and vice versa

CALCULATING IT FOR
BP

Figure 23.2 shows how the highlighted numbers from this extract of BP's accounts combine to produce the "magic number".

Figure 23.2 Calculating Free Cash Flow from BP's 1999 Accounts

The figures ...

Summary group cash flow statement	**$m**	**$m**
For the year ended 31 December	**1999**	**1998**
(p. 32 in the published accounts of BP)		
Net cash inflow from operating activities	**10,290**	**9,586**
Dividends from joint ventures	**949**	**544**
Dividends from associated undertakings	**219**	**422**
Net cash outflow from servicing of finance etc.	**−1,003**	**−825**
Tax paid	**−1,260**	**−1,705**
Net cash outflow for capital expenditure etc.	**−5,385**	**−7,298**
Net cash inflow for acquisitions and disposals	243	778
Equity dividends paid	−4,135	−2,408
Net cash outflow	−82	−906

The calculations ...

	1999	1998
Free cash flow before capital spending	**9,195**	**8,022**
(working)	(10,290 + 949 + 219 − 1,003 − 1,260)	(9,586 + 544 + 422 − 825 − 1,705)

This is cash flow from operations plus dividends from associates and joint ventures less interest and tax paid

	1999	1998
Maintenance capital spending	−3,608	−4,890
(working)	(−5,385 × 0.67)	(−7,298 × 0.67)

This is estimated at two-thirds of total capital spending

	1999	1998
Free cash flow	**5,587**	**3,132**
(working)	(9,195 − 3,608)	(8,022 − 4,890)

This figure is free cash flow before capital spending minus estimated maintenance capex

In BP's case, the calculation is fairly straightforward and can be derived without needing to resort to the notes of the accounts.

BP's summary accounts (the ones used here) contain little in the way of clues to the split between maintenance capital spending and spending on new assets. Indeed, the notes analyzing this show capital spending lumped together with spending on acquisitions. For the sake of simplicity, we assume that maintenance capital spending is around two-thirds of the total.

The large amounts of presentation material available at the company's excellent web site may also contain a clue as to the precise figure, although this was not immediately apparent from a cursory glance.

What it Means

The point about the free cash flow calculation is that it represents the amount of cash left over after all essential deductions have been made. Companies have a choice about how free cash flow is spent. It may be paid to shareholders in the form of dividends; used for acquisitions, for share buy-backs, or for straightforward "organic" capital investment in the business; or it may simply be retained.

How a company spends its free cash flow can be revealing about its view of future events. If it fears a recession, it may build cash; if it believes the economy will be strong, it may institute a share buy-back or make a big acquisition.

In this example, most of BP's cash is actually spent on shareholder dividends; nothing is spent on acquisitions after disposals are taken into account, and the balance probably goes on new capital investment.

Free cash flow is a starting point for several other "magic numbers" we will look at later, notably price to cash flow and discounted cash flow.

Magic Number

24 Fixed Asset Spending/ Depreciation

The Definition

Fixed asset spending (FAS) is usually an indicator of the degree to which a company is investing for the long-term health of the business. *Depreciation* (D) is the amount it notionally sets aside each year to replace existing fixed assets. The comparison of one to the other shows how expansion-minded management is. If fixed asset spending is double the depreciation charge, this shows the company is spending as much again to expand its asset base as it is on replacing existing assets.

The Formula

FAS/D ratio = Gross spending on fixed assets/Annual depreciation charge

The Components

Gross spending on fixed assets – this item is the annual amount spent in cash terms on fixed assets, including new property, plant, and machinery. There are circumstances that might dictate including spending on certain intangible assets (for example, software licenses, customer lists, and so on). This should only be done if they are assets that will subsequently bear a depreciation charge. Ignore proceeds from the sale of fixed assets when calculating this ratio.

Annual depreciation charge – this is the annual amount set aside to cover the replacement of fixed assets. In this calculation, you should exclude anything relating to the amortization of goodwill.

Where's the Data?

Gross spending on fixed assets – this is easily located in the cash flow statement.

Annual depreciation charge – this is normally in the cash flow statement. It also crops up as a charge in the profit and loss account note about operating expenses. If the figures differ, take the cash flow charge as the correct one. You can often find a more detailed breakdown of depreciation in the note relating to balance sheet fixed assets. The key phrase to look for here is "charge for year" under the "depreciation" heading.

Calculating it – the Theory

Figure 24.1 shows the different numbers to be extracted from the accounts and how to use them to calculate the ratio.

Figure 24.1 Calculating the "Magic Number" for ... Fixed Asset Spending/Depreciation

Universal Widgets Inc. has the following items in its cash flow statement:

	$m
Depreciation and amortization	50
Amortization of goodwill	10
Purchase of real estate, machinery, and equipment	75
Proceeds from sale of real estate and machinery	5
FAS/D is	**1.5**
(working)	(75/50)

CALCULATING IT FOR AJINOMOTO

Figure 24.2 shows how the highlighted numbers from this extract of Ajinomoto's accounts combine to produce the "magic number".

Figure 24.2 Calculating Fixed Asset Spending/Depreciation from Ajinomoto's Accounts

The figures ...

Ajinomoto and consolidated subsidiaries
years ended 31 March 2000, 1999 and 1998
(p. 31 in the published accounts of Ajinomoto)

		millions of ¥	
	2000	**1999**	**1998**
Cash flow from operations			
Income before taxes and minority interests	34,336	28,875	42,281
Depreciation and amortization	**37,334**	**33,365**	**32,029**
Amortization of excess of cost over net assts acquired	2,639	1,987	2,420
Cash flows from investing activities			
(Increase) decrease in marketable securities	−2,257	19,333	−1,603
Acquisition of property, plant, and equipment	**−46,381**	**−53,395**	**−50,077**
Proceeds from sale of property, plant, and equipment	5,389	2,623	2,232
Acquisition of intangible assets, net of proceeds	−8,511	−2,592	735

The calculation ...

	2000	1999	1998
FAS/D	**1.24**	**1.60**	**1.56**
(working)	(46,381/37,334)	(53,395/33,365)	(50,077/32,029)

In each case the calculation is a simple division of the highlighted figures, with plus and minus signs ignored

The calculation in this case is exceptionally straightforward with the figures clearly available in the company's cash flow statement. There are few accounting peculiarities to worry about.

Interpreting the results is also fairly easy. The company is consistently spending above its depreciation charge, which is good, but not excessively so, which is also good. The extent of the extra spending has been falling. This may simply be the end of a longer period of higher spending, or reflect greater caution on the part of the company's management.

WHAT IT MEANS

The example is entirely typical of the interpretation and use of the ratio in general. In itself, the ratio has limited value. If, however, it is looked at over a three- or five-year period, the numbers can be placed in their proper context. As with many other "magic numbers", comparing a company's ratio of fixed asset spending to depreciation with those of its peers may yield some insights.

A particularly good test is to compare the ratio with return on equity or return on capital employed. If these percentage returns are low, and the company is spending well above its depreciation rate, there is a good chance that the extra spending is not going to a particularly productive use. This will gradually destroy the value of the business to its shareholders.

Examine the company's depreciation policies at the same time. The policies pursued by the company can normally be found at the start of the notes to the accounts, or located from the index. Compare the depreciation policies with those of similar companies.

Do the ones for the company in question look unduly conservative or not? Judge the level of spending and the trends in it with this in mind. Look for any changes in policy in previous years that might have influenced the ratio, especially if there is a marked change in trend from one year to the next.

Finally, remember that there are companies to which this ratio does not apply, specifically those operating "people businesses". These are run with relatively low fixed assets relative to their turnover. Examples include advertising agencies, consultancy companies, software businesses, any business involved in licensing rather than manufacturing, and so on. For businesses like this, this particular "magic number" can be ignored.

Magic Number

25 Operating Cash Flow/ Operating Profit

The Definition

This ratio is calculated by dividing *cash flow from operations* (from the cash flow statement) by *operating profit* (from the income statement). In all normal circumstances, cash flow from operations should consistently exceed operating profit. In short, the ratio should exceed one.

The Formula

Ratio = Operating cash flow/Operating profit

The Components

Operating cash flow – sometimes called "net cash from operating activities" or "net cash inflow from operating activities", this figure is the result of adjusting operating profit for items that affect the way profit is calculated but do not represent movements of cash. These items include depreciation and amortization, provisions, retained profits of associated or related partly-owned companies, and changes in debtors, creditors, and stocks. Most companies show how operating cash flow is arrived at in detail.

Operating profit – sometimes called "operating income", this is found by taking gross profit and deducting various other items such as depreciation and amortization, staff costs, and sales and marketing expenditure. Those items not deducted, at least until the next stage down the income statement, are income (or losses) attributable to related companies or associates (companies that are less than 50% owned), or net interest paid or received.

Where's the Data?

Operating cash flow – this is in the cash flow statement toward the top of the page. Avoid confusing the figure for operating cash flow with operating profit (see below). Cash flow tables often start with operating profit – taken from the income statement – as the top-most figure and then show how the various adjustments produce operating cash flow. In other cases, this reconciliation of the two figures is contained in a note.

Operating profit – this is found in the income statement and is occasionally called "trading profit", although there are some subtle accounting distinctions between the two. Trading profit tends to correspond to profit before interest (sometimes called "earnings before interest and tax", or EBIT). It may include an item, say the profit on the sales of fixed asset investments, which does not relate directly to the mainstream operations of the company. Items like this should, if possible, be excluded from operating profit.

Calculating it – the Theory

Figure 25.1 shows the different numbers to be pulled from the accounts and how to use them to calculate the ratio.

Figure 25.1 Calculating the "Magic Number" for ... Operating Cash Flow/Operating Profit

Universal Widgets has the following note to its cash flow statement:

	£m
Operating profit	420
Exceptional items	−20
	400
Depreciation	300
(Increase)/decrease in stocks	−25
(Increase)/decrease in debtors	35
(Increase)/decrease in creditors	20
Increase in provisions	5
Net cash inflow from operating activities	735
Operating cash flow/Operating profit is	**1.75**
(working)	(735/420)

CALCULATING IT FOR
GREAT UNIVERSAL STORES

Figure 25.2 shows how the highlighted numbers from this extract of GUS's accounts combine to produce the "magic number".

Figure 25.2 Calculating Operating Cash Flow/Operating Profit from GUS's 2000 Accounts

The figures ...

Notes to the consolidated cash flow statement
(p. 62 in the published accounts of GUS)

(a) Net cash flow from operating activities	**2000**	**1999**
	£m	**£m**
Operating profit	**420.7**	**538.0**
Exceptional items	0	−23.7
	420.7	513.4
Depreciation	299.4	270.0
(Increase)/decrease in stocks	−26.9	57.5
(Increase)/decrease in debtors	401.3	325.6
(Increase)/decrease in creditors	52.5	−152.2
Increase in provisions for liabilities and charges	0.6	25.2
Net cash inflow from operating activities	**1,147.6**	**1,040.4**

The calculation ...

Operating cash flow/Operating profit	**2.72**	**1.93**
(working)	(1,147.6/420.7)	(1,040.4/538)

GUS's net cash inflow from operating activities is divided by operating profit before exceptional items in each case

As in the previous example, the calculation is straightforward in the case of GUS, the only minor wrinkle being the decision on whether or not to include exceptional items. It is normal to exclude them since they will inevitably distort any comparisons that may be made.

The example shows that GUS not only has substantial depreciation but also that it has, over the past two years, been able to squeeze additional cash out of the business by tightening up on its use of working capital. Working capital is the amount of money tied up in the business in stocks and unpaid bills from customers, less any unpaid bills owing to suppliers. By reducing stocks and getting faster payment of money owing from customers, companies can generate additional cash.

WHAT IT MEANS

The example shows very logically how changes in working capital and the size of the depreciation charge produce the difference between operating profit and operating cash flow. GUS's accounting layout is a model in this respect.

Not all companies are as clear as this. It is important, for example, to remember that like should be compared with like. Operating profit is simply adjusted for the non-cash items (depreciation, amortization, and provisions) that are deducted in the process of arriving at operating profit. Operating cash flow should not therefore be calculated after tax, interest, dividends, and the like, because none of these items is deducted from operating profit.

The beauty of this ratio, which effectively measures the efficiency with which profits are converted into cash, is that it is simple to calculate and speaks volumes about the efficiency of the company. Because depreciation and other non-cash charges are added back, operating cash flow should always be higher than operating profit. If it is not, it usually means there has been deterioration in working capital ratios.

Companies that have cash conversion ratios of less than 100% are on a slippery slope, generating less cash than their income statement implies. Conversely, the more the ratio exceeds 100%, the more profits are being "hidden" (perhaps by a very conservative depreciation policy) and the better the investment is likely to prove.

In addition, unlike the last "magic number", this one works for all types of companies. It is also good to compare the operating cash flow to operating profit ratio over a period of years, to make sure that the figures are consistent and not simply showing an unsustainable one-off improvement. Differences between companies generally reflect the conservatism or otherwise of management in calculating depreciation and other non-cash items, and the efficiency with which working capital is used.

Magic Number 26

Price to Free Cash Flow Ratio

The Definition

Like the price-earnings ratio ("Magic number" 3), the *price to free cash flow ratio* (PCF) compares the share price with free cash flow per share. Sometimes the cash flow figure is stated before deducting maintenance capital spending.

The Formula

PCF = Share price/(Free cash flow/Weighted average shares in issue)

The Components

Share (stock) price – the current market price of the shares, normally the mid-market price at close of business on the previous trading day.

Free cash flow – all cash flow calculations ignore book-entry transactions and concentrate purely on the flows of cash into and out of a business. Hence they ignore depreciation, amortization of goodwill, retained profits of minority-owned companies, and capitalized interest. Strictly speaking, free cash flow also deducts those items that a company cannot avoid paying if it wants to stay in business: interest, tax, and sufficient capital spending to maintain its fixed assets.

Weighted average shares in issue – the time-weighted average number of shares in issue during the year. The shares concerned are those that have been issued and are publicly listed.

Any stock splits should also be allowed for. The calculation of the weighted average is normally performed on a monthly basis. For example, the increased number of shares in issue that took place eight months into the year would have a weighting of 4/12 in the calculation (because four months of the year remain), while the original number of shares in issue at the start of the year would have a weighting of 8/12.

Where's the Data?

Share (stock) price – from any daily newspaper or financial web site.

Free cash flow – most of the components of free cash flow (operating cash flow, interest paid, tax paid) can be found in the cash flow statement. Avoid confusing the figure for operating cash flow with that for operating profit. Cash flow tables often start with operating profit as the top-most figure and then show how the various adjustments produce operating cash flow.

Capital spending is in the cash flow statement or the notes relating to it, under the heading "net cash outflow for capital expenditure, purchase of fixed assets, and financial investment" – or some combination of these words. Payments for acquisitions (usually termed "purchase of subsidiaries", and the like) and any suspiciously large one-off items can be ignored. Maintenance capital spending is generally assumed to be around half to two-thirds of total capital spending.

Weighted average shares in issue – this is generally found in the note to the accounts referring to the earnings per share calculation. Earnings per share are often calculated for investors and stated at the foot of the income statement. The note will normally say what weighted average number has been used in the calculation. The weighted average used for calculating earnings per share can be used for working out free cash flow per share.

Calculating it – the Theory

Figure 26.1 shows the different numbers to be pulled from the accounts and how to use them to calculate the ratio.

Figure 26.1 Calculating the "Magic Number" for ... Price to Free Cash Flow per Share

Universal Widgets Inc. has the following cash flow and income statement items:

	$m
Net cash inflow from operations	100
Depreciation	20
Amortization of goodwill	25
Interest paid	−15
Tax paid	−22
Purchases of fixed assets	−17
Sales of fixed assets	2
Free cash flow before capital spent	63
(working)	(100 − 15 − 22)
Maintenance capital spending	−10
(working)	two-thirds (say) of −17 + 2)
Free cash flow	53
Weighted average shares in issue	10m
Share price	$50
Free cash flow per share	$5.30
(working)	(53/10)
Price to FCF per share is	**9.4**
(working)	(50/5.30)

Calculating it for
BP

Figure 26.2 shows how the highlighted numbers from this extract of BP's accounts combine to produce the "magic number".

Figure 26.2 Calculating Price/Free to Cash Flow per Share from BP's 1999 Accounts

The figures ...

Summary group cash flow statement for the year ended 31 December (p. 32 in the published accounts of BP)	**1999**	**$m 1998**
Net cash inflow from operating activities	**10,290**	**9,586**
Dividends from joint ventures	**949**	**544**
Dividends from associated undertakings	**219**	**422**
Net cash outflow from servicing of finance etc.	**−1,003**	**−825**
Tax paid	**−1,260**	**−1,705**
Net cash outflow for capital expenditure etc.	**−5,385**	**−7,298**
Net cash inflow for acquisitions and disposals	243	778
Equity dividends paid	−4,135	−2,408
Net cash outflow	−82	−906
Weighted average shares in issue (m)	**19,396**	**19,577**

Not disclosed in summary accounts but calculated by deduction by dividing attributable profit by earnings per share

Share price at time of writing	**600p**	

The calculations ...

	1999	1998
Free cash flow before capital spending	**9,195**	**8,022**
(working)	(10,290 + 949 + 219 − 1,003 − 1,260)	(9,586 + 544 + 422 − 825 − 1,705)

This is cash flow from operations plus dividends from associates and joint ventures less interest and tax paid

Maintenance capital spending	−3,608	−4,890
(working)	(−5,385 × 0.67)	(−7,298 × 0.67)

This is estimated at two-thirds of total capital spending

Free cash flow	**5,587**	**3,132**
(working)	(9,195 − 3,608)	(8,022-4,890)

This is free cash flow before capital spending minus estimated maintenance capex

Free cash flow per share	**28.8p**	**16.0p**
(working)	(5,587/19,396)	(3,132/19,577)

This is free cash flow divided by weighted average shares in issue

Price to free cash flow ratio	**20.8 times**
(working)	(600/28.8)

This is price divided by free cash flow per share

This takes the figure introduced in "Magic number" 23 a little further on, adding in weighted average shares in issue – necessary to calculate cash flow per share. It then divides the result by the share price of 600p.

The only minor wrinkle is in the estimation of BP's weighted average shares in issue for the year in question. These do not appear to be explicitly disclosed in the summary accounts used.

These can, however, be calculated by dividing attributable profit by earnings per share, using two of the normal components of the EPS calculation to arrive at the third missing one.

What it Means

Like the price-earnings ratio (PER), PCF is a key ratio for analysts and investors alike. One way of looking at it is that it represents the number of years of free cash flow at the current rate before the price of the shares is recouped. This idea is notional since the cash flow will not be returned in full to shareholders.

Like the PER too, the important aspect of the PCF is that it enables companies to be compared irrespective of their size, the concept reducing each company to a common currency. This is important because it will, for example, enable the stock market rating of an individual company to be compared with its competitors, and with the market.

Prospective (that is, forecast) cash flows are often used to calculate the PCF. Although less widely studied than earnings or sales revenues, the market sets some store by these predictions. As we noted earlier, one reason why stock market analysts are paid the huge amounts they are is because of a supposed skill in forecasting. However, various factors conspire to make cash flow per share less predictable than earnings per share, and the growth trend in cash flow may be more erratic than earnings for reasons that may lie outside the control of the company.

The virtue of free cash flow is, however, that it is a more objective measure of the worth of a company, less liable to be "fudged" or "smoothed". Changes in accounting policies, and not least the ingenuity of analysts in manipulating earnings calculations to suit the case they wish to make, do mean that cash flow per share is increasingly being seen as a more reliable means of judging whether a company is undervalued or overvalued.

And, as seen in "Magic number" 30, there are other ways in which free cash flow can be used to work out the "correct" price for a company's shares.

Part Five

Risk, Return, and Volatility "Magic Numbers"

Risk, Return, and Volatility "Magic Numbers"

Each of the seven "magic numbers" contained in this part looks at the inter-relationships between an investment's value, the returns it can generate, and its inherent risk.

As we remarked at the start of this book, confusing price with value is one of the biggest mistakes you can make in investing. The other is to look at returns without assessing the risk, or the potential volatility, of an investment.

Simply because an investment has a big return does not necessarily mean it is a bargain. The return may come with an undue amount of risk attached. By the same token, an investment with a lower return, but little risk, may suit some investors.

Allied to these ideas is the concept of "discounting". This is the mechanism by which you assess the current worth of a return that may come some years in the future. The risk-free rate of return, which is derived from public information on government bond yields, is central to all of these concepts.

The "magic numbers" outlined in the following pages are the tools to help you get to grips with these concepts:

- Redemption yields on government bonds are universally used both as a way of determining the risk-free rate of return (used in later calculations) and as a measure of credit quality.
- The internal rate of return (IRR) reconciles the cash invested in an asset at various different times and in different amounts with the eventual proceeds from its sale, the result expressed as a compound annual rate of return.
- Weighted average cost of capital (WACC) calculates the cost of a company's various types of capital (equity and debt) in terms of their "opportunity cost" and relative risk. From this you can assess whether or not the returns being earned by the company are adequate.
- Reinvested return on equity uses ROE, and the proportion of profits retained, to project a future value for a company and, by comparing

this figure with the current market value of the company, can show whether its shares are cheap or expensive.

- Discounted cash flow (DCF) does the reverse. It predicts a future stream of cash, and discounts successive years back to the present. The numbers are then totaled and compared with the current value of the company.
- Volatility shows how much the price of an asset (shares, bonds, funds) varies from its long-term average. It is often taken to be a proxy for the relative risk of holding an asset.
- The Sharpe ratio is a way of adjusting investment returns to allow for both the risk-free rate of return and the volatility of the underlying investment.

These "magic numbers" represent some of the more esoteric ways in which investments are valued. But they are extremely useful for investors. Each has its own importance and can be given more or less weight depending on the type of investment being valued.

Redemption yields are universally used as a way of assessing the relative merits of bonds, for predicting interest rate movements, and for working out the relative risk of default of different issuers.

Internal rates of return are often used to value private equity investments.

The WACC is used in enterprise value analysis, and the equity risk premium also plays a part in the DCF calculations.

Reinvested ROE is typically used to compare high-growth, high-return companies, to see whether or not their exalted stock market ratings are justified.

DCF is used for evaluating companies whose cash flow growth is reasonably regular and predictable. It can often highlight unexpected undervaluation.

Volatility is extensively used in pricing equity and index options, and as a component of the Sharpe ratio.

The Sharpe ratio is often used to assess the relative merits of hedge funds and hedge fund styles, but can equally be used to compare shares and indices' performance.

Read on for the inside track on these final seven "magic numbers" …

Magic Number 27

Redemption Yield/ Risk-free Rate of Return

The Definition

The *redemption yield* is sometimes called "yield to maturity" (or simply YTM). It is a concept that applies to bonds, but it also has applications in stock investing.

The redemption yield has three components: (1) the "running" (or interest yield) on a bond; (2) interest-on-interest that would be earned if successive interest payments were reinvested; and (3) the annual rate of capital gain or loss that would be made if a bond were held until maturity and repaid at its issue (or "par") value.

The Formula

YTM = Running yield + "Interest-on-interest" + Gain or loss on maturity

The Components

Coupon – this is the stated interest rate on the bond. Bonds are usually described in terms like "5% Treasury stock 2004". The coupon on the bond in this case is 5%.

Net price – the current price of the bond. Par value is normally 100%, and bonds are usually priced in percentages relative to this figure. A bond standing below par might be priced at, say, 95 (or 95%). The percent sign is usually omitted.

Market prices are stated net of any interest that has accrued since the last interest date, but this is added to, or subtracted from, dealing prices for buyers/sellers as appropriate. There are several different conventions for calculating accrued interest. This extra element in the price paid by the buyer is to compensate the seller for forgoing his or her rights to the appropriate part of the next payment.

Interest-on-interest – if a bond's periodic interest payments were reinvested, the reinvested money would also begin to earn interest. In practice, only professional investors investing in bonds on a large scale will do this, but the interest-on-interest component can be a significant element of the redemption yield on a long-term bond.

Running yield – the price of the bond expressed as a percentage of the market price. If the bond stands above par, the running yield will be less than the coupon, and vice versa.

Maturity date and par value – if a bond matures in four years' time, currently stands at 95, and has a par value (or value at redemption) of 100, it might be assumed to appreciate at 1.25% a year between now and its maturity date.

Where's the Data?

Coupon, maturity, and net price – bond details in newspapers and financial web sites usually state all three elements. The precise month and day of redemption should be checked, as should the frequency of interest payments.

Running yield – this is calculated by expressing the coupon as a percentage of the price. A bond with a 5% coupon standing at 95 has a running yield of 5.263% (5 × 100/95). Newspapers usually carry running yield information alongside redemption yield data.

Calculating it – the Theory

Figure 27.1 shows how the redemption yield can be calculated in a fictional example. Because the calculation is complex, redemption yields are calculated using either a financial calculator or a specialized book of tables, reading across from the appropriate maturity, and coupons for a given price. Financial calculators now have the facility to calculate redemption yields.

Figure 27.1 Calculating the "Magic Number" for ... Redemption Yield

A government bond has:

A coupon of 5.00%
The deal settles on .... 15 April 1999
The bond is redeemed at 100 on .... 3 September 2000
Its price is .... 96.84 + accrued interest of 0.58

Using a Texas Instruments BAII plus
financial calculator, **the yield to maturity is** **7.44%**

In other words, the current running yield of 5.16% is supplemented by the gain in price from 97.42 (net price plus accrued interest) to 100 over a period of approximately 16.5 months

CALCULATING IT FOR
5% TREASURY STOCK 2004

Figure 27.2 shows how the numbers related to this British Government stock combine to produce the "magic number".

Figure 27.2 Calculating Yield to Maturity for 5% Treasury Stock 2004

The figures ...

This UK "gilt-edge" stock, denominated in pounds sterling, has:

A coupon of	5%
Interest paid on	7 June and 7 December
Matures on	7 June 2004
Matures at	100
A net price of	100.37
Accrued interest of 22 days	0.3
The deal is executed on	20 December 2000
The deal settles on	28 December 2000

The calculations ...

There are several good online bond calculators that perform the job done by a normal financial calculator. A good example is shown in the screen shot and can be accessed online at *www.calculatorweb.com*

There is a link to it at *www.magicnumbersbook.com*

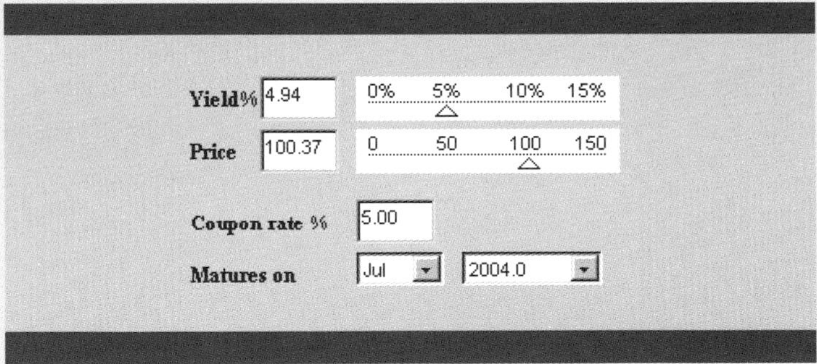

Moving the sliders to the desired values will enable you to compare price and yield changes dynamically

As can be seen, this produces a redemption yield close to but not identical to the running yield, because of the closeness of price to the par value of 100

In practice, bond redemption yields (always counted gross – that is, before any withholding tax on dividends or capital) can be found from a financial newspaper or web site, but it is important to be aware of the nature of the components that go to make up the yield. Because in some markets income and capital may be taxed at different rates, even if they have the same gross redemption yield, one type of bond may be preferred over another for tax reasons.

What it Means

Bond yields are the basis for many other financial calculations. Redemption yields on government bonds have three major uses:

(1) *As an indicator of economic health.* Bonds with less time to run to maturity stand on lower yields than those that have redemption dates further in the future. This is because investors would rather have money now or a short time in the future than wait longer for it. This relationship between yields of bonds of lengthening redemption dates is called the "yield curve". At certain times (as is the case in the UK in 2001), instead of sloping up from left to right, the yield curve slopes the other way. Shorter-term rates are higher than longer-term ones. This is usually considered to be a sign of an imminent recession.

(2) *As a measure of the risk-free rate of return.* G7 governments are highly unlikely to default on their debt. Invest in their bonds, and there is virtually guaranteed repayment of capital – at the par value – on maturity. The yield to maturity is therefore an indicator of what the market views as the annual risk-free rate of return for that period of time. This concept is often used to establish a rate at which to discount future profits, dividends, and cash flow.

(3) *As a measure of credit quality.* US "Treasuries" are, by convention, the benchmark against which all other bonds are measured. The difference between yields of bonds of the same maturity is known as the "spread" (or occasionally "basis") and is usually measured in basis points where one basis point ("bp") represents one-hundredth of 1%. Hence, a bond yielding 7% when the comparable US Treasury yielded 5% would have a spread of 200 bp.

Spreads allow investors to establish a pecking order between bonds, as determined by the market. A bond's standing in the pecking order depends on several factors: the perceived risk of default; the currency in which the bond is denominated and the prospects for it (prospects of a strong currency might increase a bond's attractiveness and therefore reduce its spread); and the likely rate of inflation in the country concerned – which is another side of the same coin.

All this talk of risk-free rates should not lead investors to imagine that bonds are intrinsically risk-free themselves. Bond prices move up and down in an inverse relationship to interest rates, since the latter influences yield expectations and hence bond prices.

Equally, because the return of a bond held to maturity is fixed and predictable, inflation is the big enemy of bonds. Bonds do best when prospects for company profits and, hence, the outlook for equities is worsening, and when there is deflationary pressure rather than inflation. In these circumstances, bank interest rates will be very low indeed and bonds will very much be the best home for money.

Magic Number

28

Internal Rate of Return

The Definition

Internal rate of return (IRR) calculates the overall annual percentage rate of return on an investment, especially where several different variables are involved.

In the case of bonds, the redemption yield is an internal rate of return. It takes into account variables such as periodic interest payments, the price paid, the time to maturity, and the price at redemption (see "Magic number" 27).

Normally, however, the IRR is used to express the return required to equate the cost of an investment (especially one bought in instalments or that generates irregular amounts of income) with the proceeds when it is sold.

In its simplest form, where a single purchase and a single sale are made, and no income is received in the meantime, the IRR is the compound annual rate of return calculated from the buying price to the sale price.

The Formula and its Components

At its simplest, the formula for IRR involves a compound growth calculation, which can be performed using compound interest tables or a financial calculator. In the case of more complex calculations, involving irregularly timed investments, periodic income, and irregular sale proceeds (or any combination of these), you can do the calculation using a specialist spreadsheet or software program.

In this case, the information required is: the timing and amounts of the investments made; the timing and amount of any income received during the life of the investment; and the timing and amount of the sale proceeds. When using IRR calculators, care has to be taken to input the amounts with the correct sign (investments are usually preceded by a minus sign, income and sale proceeds, and income receipts with a plus). If this rule is not followed, an error will result.

Where's the Data?

A simple online IRR calculator that illustrates the principles described above is at *www.jamesko.com/irr.asp*. A link to this site is also at *www.magicnumbersbook.com*. The calculator is self-explanatory, and a more flexible and complex version of the product is available for purchase.

Calculating It

Figure 28.1 shows a spreadsheet giving a matrix of IRR values for different time periods and different multiples of the original investment. The table assumes a single investment, a single sale, and no income received in the meantime.

Figure 28.1 Calculating IRR ... A Ready Reckoner

IRR (%)

Multiple of original investment returned/ Years	2 ×	2.5 ×	3 ×	3.5 ×	4 ×	5 ×	6×	8 ×	10 ×
2	41	58	73	87	100	124	145	183	216
3	26	36	44	52	59	71	82	100	115
4	19	26	32	37	41	49	56	68	78
5	15	20	25	28	32	38	43	52	58
6	12	16	20	23	26	31	35	41	47
7	10	14	17	20	22	26	29	35	39
8	9	12	15	17	19	22	25	30	33
9	8	11	13	15	17	20	22	26	29
10	7	10	12	13	15	17	20	23	26

Example: An investment that returned three times the original investment over four years would have an IRR of 32%

One that returned double the original investment over nine years would produce an IRR of 8%

This spreadsheet can also be downloaded from *www.magicnumbers-book.com*. It can be used to derive an approximate IRR, but a more accurate calculation can be performed using the online calculator mentioned previously. Figure 28.2 shows the difference between the two approaches.

Figure 28.2 Calculating IRR for Universal Widgets

You have made an investment in Universal Widgets Pte, committing S$12 million in year 1. You receive dividends of S$1 million in year 3, and sell the investment for S$37 million in year 7.

Method One – Using the Ready Reckoner

Assume you invested S$12 million at the outset, and received S$38 million (proceeds plus dividends) in year 7

Reading from the ready reckoner:

The investment has run for six years (year 1 to year 7)

The multiple received is 3.17 times (38/12)

The IRR is therefore *slightly over 20%*

Method Two – Using the Online Calculator

The result of this method is shown in the screengrab.

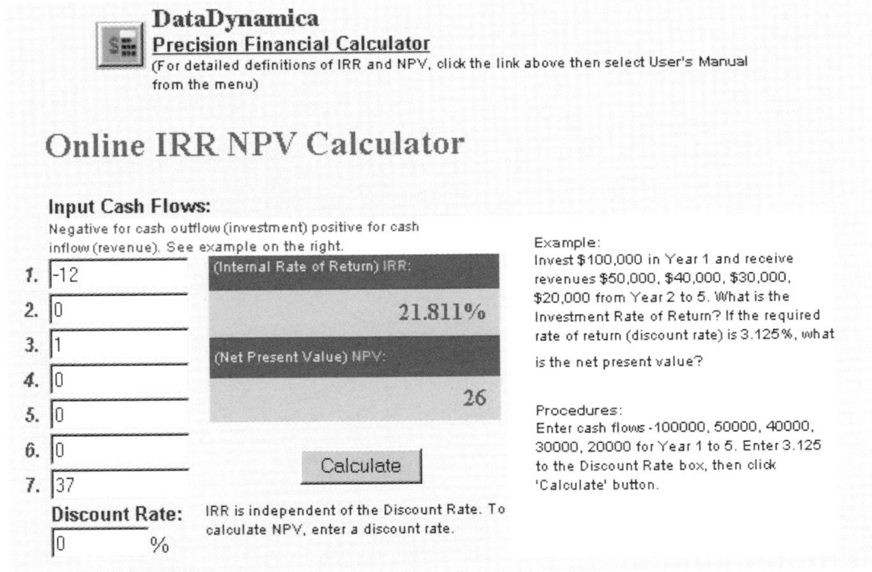

The resulting *IRR is 21.81%*

The greater precision of the software-based calculation is obvious but the ready reckoner also gives a reasonably accurate result!

What it Means

IRRs are invariably used by venture capitalists to assess the worth of an investment. In this instance, venture capitalists will have a target IRR and often work back from a calculation of what is a feasible "exit price" to determine whether or not the required amount of investment required can be justified – allowing for various ways in which a deal can be structured.

IRR can also be applied to the calculation for reinvested return on equity (see "Magic number" 31) when calculating the compound return implied by an investment.

The goal with IRR is to achieve a rate of return that, to compensate for the risks involved, substantially exceeds the return that could be earned from a risk-free investment.

Magic Number

29 Weighted Average Cost of Capital

The Definition

Weighted average cost of capital (WACC, and sometimes called the "composite cost of capital") is usually compared with the actual return on capital earned by a company to work out how much value (if any) management is adding for shareholders.

The calculation "weights" the cost of equity with the percentage share that equity represents in the capital structure, and the cost of debt with the percentage share it represents, to produce a composite figure.

Calculating the cost of equity is not as simple as it might seem. Contrary to what you might think, it is not simply a function of, for example, the dividend yield on the shares. Rather, it is the opportunity cost of investing in the equity, taking account of the inherent risks involved.

The Formula

$$\text{WACC} = \text{Cost of equity} \times (\text{Market capitalization/Enterprise value}) + \text{Cost of debt (Debt/Enterprise value)}$$

The Components

Cost of equity – as explained already, this is a difficult figure to calculate because it depends on several other complex variables. Expressed in plain language, the cost of equity is the risk-free rate of return plus the "equity risk premium" adjusted for the "systemic risk" involved in the equity.

Risk-free rate of return – this is typically the redemption yield on a high-quality government bond.

Equity risk premium – this is the amount by which, typically, the return on equities exceeds the risk-free rate of return over the longer term.

Systemic risk (*sometimes called "beta"*) – this is the degree to which the shares in question are more or less volatile than the market as a whole. A share with a beta of 1.2 would rise 12% if the market rose 10%, other things being equal, or fall 12% if the market fell 10%. Shares with betas of less than one are considered to have less risk (in other words, are less volatile) than those with betas of more than one, and warrant a lower equity risk premium. Statistically, beta is calculated by performing a regression analysis on the movements in the share price versus those of the market.

Cost of equity – this is always calculated as a monetary value.

Cost of debt – this is the monetary value that equates to the yield to maturity on the company's debt, since this will represent the market's view of the risk of the debt relative to a risk-free band.

Market capitalization – this is the stock market value of the company and is calculated by multiplying the total of issued shares (or common stock) outstanding by their price.

Enterprise value (*often abbreviated to EV*) – this is a measure that adjusts the market capitalization for the balance of any cash or debt the company may have. If a company has more debt than cash, the market capitalization is increased by the difference between the two numbers. If cash exceeds debt, enterprise value is reduced by the difference.

Where's the Data?

Cost of equity – there are various studies that examine the long-term equity risk premium. One of the most readily available is the annual equity-gilt study published by the investment bank Credit Suisse First Boston (CSFB), which examines the phenomenon over an extended period of time. The report can be downloaded from *www.csfb.com.* Barclays Capital (*www.barcap.com*) also produces a similar report each year. Most estimates put the equity risk premium in the US at between 4% and 7.5% depending on the time period chosen. In the UK, according to the CSFB study, 6.5% to 8% is appropriate.

In the case of beta for individual companies, some investment software packages contain estimates of it, as do reference publications published by leading business schools.

Cost of debt – this is calculated, for listed debt, on the basis of the redemption yield of the security in question. For all other debt, the interest cost in the cash flow statement (less the interest paid on listed debt, where the other calculation is used) is the best proxy, calculating the cost as a percentage of the principal amount in question.

Enterprise value and market value – refer to "Magic numbers" 1 and 2.

CALCULATING IT

Figure 29.1 shows how to calculate the ratio using a hypothetical example.

Figure 29.1 Calculating the "Magic Number" for ... Weighted Average Cost of Capital

Universal Widgets Inc. has the following attributes (together with relevant market parameters):

Risk-free rate of return (30-year US Treasuries)	5.43%
Equity risk premium	4.10%
Beta factor	1.4
Redemption yield on debt	6.30%
Amount of debt	$200m
Market capitalization	$800m
Adjusted risk premium is	**5.74%**
(working)	(4.1 × 1.4)
Percentage cost of equity is	**11.17%**
(working)	(5.43% + 5.74%)
Absolute cost of equity is	**$89.36m**
(working)	(11.17 × 800)
Absolute cost of debt is	**$12.6m**
(working)	(6.3 × 200)
WACC is	**10.20%**
(working)	(89.36 + 12.6) × 100/(800 + 200)

The steps in the calculation can be seen clearly. The beta factor of 1.4 increases the equity risk premium. When added to the risk-free rate of return, this suggests an opportunity cost of investing in the equity of around 11.2%. The cost of debt is based on the redemption yield, and the two components weighted according to the proportions they represent of total enterprise value.

Because of the difficulty of estimating the equity risk premium and the beta for individual stocks, we have not calculated this figure for a "live" example.

WHAT IT MEANS

In reality, the calculations are likely to be much more complicated than the example suggests, since minority interests must be taken into account, as must any preference shares, and any other aspects of the corporate capital structure.

However, the significance of WACC lies less in how it is calculated than in how it is used.

In the hypothetical example of Universal Widgets, it is clear that if the company were not earning an after-tax return on capital greater than 9%, then investors in the shares would be better off elsewhere. In other words, management's use of the capital placed at their disposal would actually result in a destruction of value for shareholders.

There are wrinkles in the calculation. It is sensitive to the assumptions made about the equity risk premium. The beta factor can be estimated with a degree of precision from the pattern of the share price relative to movements in the market, but the equity risk premium varies from market to market and over time.

Yet the calculation of the risk-adjusted cost of equity has interesting applications in other calculations, notably where an element of discounting is involved. In a discounted cash flow calculation, looked at in the next section, one key variable that can be chosen by the user is the rate at which future cash flows are discounted. The options are to use the risk-free rate of return or one that is "risk-adjusted" for beta and the equity risk premium.

Magic Number 30

Discounted Cash Flow

The Definition

Discounted cash flow (DCF) is a way of valuing companies by forecasting cash flow for a period of years into the future and applying a discount factor to each year's figure to reflect the expected time until it accrues. The further in the future, the greater the discount applied to that year's cash flow. The discounted cash flows for each of the years are then added together, an additional value placed on the total cash expected to accrue beyond that, and the total compared with the market value of the company.

The Formula

DCF = Free cash flow year 1 × (d year 1) … etc… + Free cash flow year 10 × (d year 10) + PV of "perpetuity"

(d = the discount factor for each year as determined by the chosen discount rate)

The Components

Free cash flow (FCF) – this is operating profit ignoring book-entry transactions. It concentrates purely on the flows of cash into and out of a business and ignores depreciation, amortization of goodwill, retained profits of minority-owned companies, capitalized interest, and any other items that are merely the result of accounting conventions. FCF also deducts those items that a company cannot avoid paying if it wants to stay in business: interest, tax, and sufficient capital spending to maintain its fixed assets. See "Magic number" 23 for more details on how to calculate it.

Forecast growth rates in cash flow – starting from FCF for the latest reported year, you need to predict how this figure will grow each year for the next ten years, or to make a conservative assumption about such growth. This is at your discretion.

"Steady state" growth rate – this is used to calculate the value of the residual cash flow estimated from year ten onwards. You would normally choose a figure less than the discount rate. A good assumption is to plug in an estimate of the long-term rate of inflation, or assume that today's rate will hold for the foreseeable future.

Discount rate – this is the rate at which the future cash flows are discounted, each successive year's cash flow reduced by an amount (the discount factor) reflecting the compounded discount rate. The discount factor reflects both investors' preference for cash sooner rather than later and the greater uncertainty (and vulnerability to subsequent inflation) of cash received in the future.

As a minimum, the discount rate should be the risk-free rate of return on ten-year money – reflecting that cash flows are usually predicted and discounted for up to ten years ahead. To be conservative, add an equity risk premium to the discount rate. Risk-free rate of return is explained in "Magic number" 27, and equity risk premium in "Magic number" 29.

Where's the Data?

Free cash flow – you can find operating cash flow and the other adjustments in the cash flow statement. Avoid confusing the figure for operating cash flow with that for operating profit. Cash flow tables often start with operating profit as the top-most figure and then show how the various adjustments produce operating cash flow. See "Magic number" 23 for more details.

Forecast growth rates and "steady state" growth rate – to be estimated by you. Historic growth rates can be used as a guide. The steady state growth rate must be less than the discount rate.

Discount rate – this is the risk-free rate of return on ten-year money, which equates, as explained in "Magic number" 27, to the yield to maturity on the benchmark ten-year government bond for the country in question. You can add in an equity risk premium. Data on equity risk premiums are sketchy. The long-term average for the UK is said to be 5.2%. You should probably use a minimum of 3% for even the least volatile stocks. If the yield on the ten-year bond is, say, 4% and the risk premium used is 5%, the discount rate would be 9% (4 + 5).

CALCULATING IT – THE THEORY

Figure 30.1 shows the different numbers to be extracted from the accounts and other sources used to calculate the ratio. Fortunately, the whole process can be computerized and the numbers plugged into a relatively simple spreadsheet. This spreadsheet can be downloaded from *www.magicnumbersbook.com*.

Figure 30.1 Calculating the "Magic Number" for ... Discounted Cash Flow

Small but rapidly developing, Widget Properties, DCF spreadsheet looks like this:

Projected	**2001**	**2002**	**2003**	**2004**	**2005**	**2006**	**2007**	**2008**	**2009**	**2010**
Prior year cash flow	300	600	900	1,125	1,238	1,361	1,497	1,617	1,714	1,783
Increase %	*100.0%*	*50.0%*	*25.0%*	*10.0%*	*10.0%*	*10.0%*	*8.0%*	*6.0%*	*4.0%*	*4.0%*
Cash flow	600	900	1,125	1,238	1,361	1,497	1,617	1,714	1,783	1,854
Discounted cash flow	555	770	890	906	921	937	936	918	883	849
Sum of discounted Cash flows		8,566								
10-year per share cash flow	£ 0.33									
Residual value										
Cash flow in year 10	1,854									
Second-stage growth rate	*2.5%*									
Cash flow in year 11	1,900									
Capitalization	5.6%									
Company value at end of year 10		33,814								
Present value of Future cash flow		22,385								
Shares (in thousands)	*25,975*									
Present value per share		**£ 0.86**								

Assumptions and notes

1 Base cash flow calculated as attributable profit plus depreciation and deferred tax less maintenance capex.

2 Discount rate assumed to be the benchmark bond yield of 5.12% plus a risk premium of 3.0%.

The figure reproduced here looks slightly different to the downloaded spreadsheet. The spreadsheet file itself contains instructions on how to use it. But remember that to use this worksheet it is not necessary to fill in any historic figures other than those for the most recent year.

Alternatively, the spreadsheet formulas can be over-ridden and the free cash flow figure calculated separately and plugged into the top left box of the forecast rows (as shown in Figure 30.1). You then enter the projected rates of increases in cash flow for the ten forward years and for the "second-stage" phase of growth.

These figures can be tailored to take into account assumptions about the timing of growth or decline that is specific to the company, or those that might be produced by the impact of the economic cycle. You need also to enter the total number of shares issued, as well as the appropriate discount rate and the current year-end date. The model calculates everything else. The year-end and discount rate used are changed using the "Entry" tab in the spreadsheet file.

CALCULATING IT FOR

NTT

Figure 30.2 shows how the highlighted numbers from NTT's accounts and various additional assumptions combine to produce the "magic number".

Figure 30.2 Calculating Discounted Cash Flow for NTT

Projected	**2001**	**2002**	**2003**	**2004**	**2005**	**2006**	**2007**	**2008**	**2009**	**2010**
Prior year cash flow	1,621	1,702	1,787	1,877	1,970	2,069	2,172	2,281	2,395	2,515
Increase %	*5.0%*	*5.0%*	*5.0%*	*5.0%*	*5.0%*	*5.0%*	*5.0%*	*5.0%*	*5.0%*	*5.0%*
Cash flow	1,702	1,787	1,877	1,970	2,069	2,172	2,281	2,395	2,515	2,640
Discounted cash flow	1,596	1,571	1,547	1,523	1,499	1,476	1,453	1,431	1,409	1,387
Sum of discounted cash flows		14,893								
10-year per share cash flow	**0.94**									
Residual value										
Cash flow in year 10	–									
Second-stage growth rate	*3%*									
Cash flow in year 11	–									
Capitalization	4%									
Company value at end of year 10	–									
Present value of future cash flow		8,601								
Shares (in thousands)	*15,835*									
Present value per share (¥)	**543**									

Assumptions and notes

1 Base cash flow calculated as attributable profit plus depreciation and deferred tax less maintenance capex.

2 Discount rate assumed to be a benchmark bond yield of 1.65% plus a risk premium of 5.0%.

NTT's discounted cash flow ascribes a value of ¥543,000 to the shares on the assumptions stated. The price of the shares at the time of writing was ¥822,000.

There are several areas where different assumptions can be made, most notably (in this instance) in the discount rate used. The risk-free rate of return for Japanese equities is low, because of low yields on Japanese government bonds – only 1.65% for the ten years, for example. In addition, NTT's equity risk premium is probably on the low side, so to use a discount rate of 6.65% may be unduly conservative.

There is another way of interpreting the figures. Use trial and error inputting different discount rates into the model. By observing the resulting effects on the present value figure in the model, you can work out the discount rate that exactly equates the discounted cash flows to the current share price. You can then make a judgment as to whether or not this is reasonable. In the case of NTT, that figure is around 4.1% – implying a risk premium of 2.45%.

What it Means

Discounted cash flow is a long-established technique originally developed for use by companies assessing capital investment projects, and has been used in the past by corporate financiers in determining valuations of companies that are potential bid targets.

The technique does, however, involve a lot of subjectivity in assessing future rates of growth. It has the merit that it is projecting forward from cash flow figures rather than, as analysts normally do, from a set of profit figures. Profits may not tell an accurate story.

Using a market yield as the basis for discount factors is also less subjective than projecting forward from assumptions about likely individual price-earnings ratios and dividend yields. It is also useful in comparing valuations across companies in a relatively stable sector (such as brewing, food retailing, and stores) where similar underlying growth rates can be reasonably confidently assumed.

The beauty of DCF models is that the figure and assumptions in them can be updated when, for example, new annual accounts are issued, when bond yields and therefore discount factors change, and when other new information comes to light.

The spreadsheet used here is one based on the principles outlined in Robert Hagstrom's book, *The Warren Buffett Way* (John Wiley & Sons). US investment guru Bob Costa devised the spreadsheet. Unfortunately, Costa's web site has been absorbed into a larger entity, but a copy of the spreadsheet is available at *www.magicnumbersbook.com*. To use it, you will need Microsoft Excel 5 or higher.

Using DCF models is a good way of getting a handle on whether a particular share represents good value or not. For obvious reasons, it works less well with cyclical stocks, recovery situations, or companies that do not have a particularly predictable pattern of sales growth.

Magic Number

31 Reinvested Return on Equity

The Definition

Reinvested return on equity (ROE) attempts to project forward the future value of a company, based on return on equity (see "Magic number" 20), dividend cover ("Magic number" 12), the risk-free rate of return ("Magic number" 27), and internal rate of return ("Magic number" 28). It is worth re-reading these sections to make sure you understand the underlying concepts and how to calculate them.

The Formula

The formula is best suited to a spreadsheet application. The reinvested ROE spreadsheet can be downloaded from *www.magicnumbersbook.com*.

It works like this. Average return on equity is calculated and adjusted to reflect the proportion of profits retained. This is used to calculate a year five value for the company, based on profits implied from the growth generated in shareholders' equity.

A market multiple is then applied to year five profits to arrive at the year five company value. After factoring in the value of dividends over the period, this is compared with the current market capitalization. A compound rate of return is calculated that equates the two. For a sufficient margin of safety to be present in the investment, this return should probably be at least 25% per annum.

The Components

Return on equity – after-tax profits expressed as a percentage of average shareholders' funds (including accumulated goodwill). See the relevant section of "Magic number" 20 for more information on how to calculate it. A company's percentage return on equity is a key measure of its ability to continue to produce high returns in the future.

The higher the return and the higher the percentage retained for reinvestment, the more cash is put to work to earn these returns in successive years, and the greater the intrinsic value of the company in the future.

Retention rate – this is calculated by subtracting dividends from after-tax profit and dividing by after-tax profits. If a company has profits of 10p a share and pays 2.5p out in dividends, it is retaining 7.5p (10.0 − 2.5) and its retention rate is therefore 75%.

Capitalization rate – this is the rate used to multiply year five projected profits to get to the projected company value in that year. The rate can be established from some form of benchmark yield (the capitalization rate would simply be the reciprocal of the yield), or else it can be chosen on some other basis, perhaps the company's current earnings multiple, or a sector or market multiple.

If a yield-based yardstick is used, the obvious choices are the risk-free rate of return (the redemption yield on a five-year benchmark government bond, for example), or a risk-adjusted rate of return calculated – for instance – by adjusting this yield for the volatility of the stock relative to the market. Volatility is discussed in more detail in "Magic number" 32.

Where's the Data?

See "Magic numbers" 20 and 12 relating to return on equity and dividend cover, respectively.

Calculating it – the Theory

Valuing companies using reinvested return on equity is an easy idea to grasp and is again susceptible to spreadsheet analysis. A spreadsheet that enables you to do this calculation is available for downloading at *www.magicnumbersbook.com*.

With this, you can extract a few figures from a company's report and accounts, make a small judgment here and there, and use the spreadsheet to produce a good guide as to whether a company's shares are good value or not.

Figure 31.1 shows the different numbers to be extracted from the accounts and how to use them in the spreadsheet.

Figure 31.1 Calculating the "Magic Number" for ... Reinvested ROE

Universal Widgets has various relevant balance sheet and income statement parameters as shown below:

Latest year-end		**Dec-00**
Historic shareholders' funds (£m)		110.00
Average shareholders' funds (£m)		100.00
Historic after-tax profit (£m)		25.00
Historic dividends (£m)		6.50
Historic ROE (%)		25.00
Retention rate		0.74
Reinvestment ROE (%)		18.50
Shareholders ... (£m)	**Equity**	**Dividends**
Year 1	130.35	8.47
Year 2	154.46	10.04
Year 3	183.04	11.90
Year 4	216.90	14.10
Year 5	257.03	16.71
Total	**61.22**	
Year 5 PAT (£m)	**64.26**	
Benchmark yield (%)	5.4	
Implied multiple	18.52	
Capitalized year 5 PAT (£m)	1,189.96	
Total return incl. divs (£m)	1,251.17	
Current mkt cap. (£m)	450.00	
% uplift/"margin of safety"	178.04	
Implied % compound return	22%	

The items in italics are those that the user needs to enter. The rest are calculated automatically.

To recap on why Figure 31.1 looks as it does:

Historic return on equity (ROE) is calculated. This is done by dividing after-tax profit by average shareholders' funds and expressing the result as a percentage.

The model works out the retention rate. It is the percentage of profits left over after dividends have been paid.

The reinvestment rate of return is calculated by multiplying ROE by the retention rate.

Profits are then compounded at this rate for five years. Dividends are assumed to rise in proportion.

The year five after-tax profit is calculated either by grossing up the dividend in year five by the retention rate, or by applying the historic ROE figure to the year five shareholders' equity figure. The result is the same either way.

Year five after-tax profit is then multiplied by the capitalization rate and the resulting figure added to accumulated dividends to arrive at a year five value for the company.

This is compared with the current market capitalization to establish the percentage annual return required to equate one to the other, or, put another way, the long-term cheapness (or lack of it) implied by the current market price of the shares.

The implied rate of return can be calculated either from compound interest tables or by using a financial calculator.

As can be seen, in this case, the result is a projected rate of return in the low 20s. This would barely be sufficient to justify investing.

CALCULATING IT FOR

SAN MIGUEL

Figure 31.2 shows how the highlighted numbers from this extract from the accounts of San Miguel combine to produce the "magic number". San Miguel is a major brewing business based in The Philippines. More information is available from its web site at *www.sanmiguel.com.ph.*

Figure 31.2 Calculating Reinvested Return on Equity for San Miguel

San Miguel has various relevant balance sheet and income statement parameters as shown below

Latest year-end		Dec-99
Historic shareholders' funds (PHPbn)		55.73
Average shareholders' funds (PHPbn)		61.37
Historic after-tax profit (PHPbn)		6.02
Historic dividends (PHPbn)		2.76
Historic ROE (%)		9.81
Retention rate		0.54
Reinvestment ROE (%)		5.31
Shareholders ... (PHPbn)	**Equity**	**Dividends**
Year 1	58.69	2.64
Year 2	61.81	2.78
Year 3	65.09	2.93
Year 4	68.55	3.08
Year 5	72.19	3.25
Total		**14.68**
Year 5 PAT (PHPbn)		**7.08**
Benchmark yield (%)		5.4
Implied multiple		18.52
Capitalized year 5 PAT (PHPbn)		131.14
Total return incl. divs (PHPbn)		145.81
Current mkt cap. (PHPbn)		126.99
% uplift/"margin of safety"		14.8
Implied % compound return		2.8

The items in italics are those that the user needs to enter. The rest are calculated automatically

San Miguel has a relatively low reinvested ROE and, assuming a multiple based around the risk-free rate of return on US Treasuries, this produces a projected year five value for the company of PHP 146 billion. The current market value of San Miguel is PHP 126.99 billion.

What it means

The advantages of an approach like this are that it is comparatively simple to calculate and that it gives due weight to the importance of return on equity in generating value for shareholders, which many other methods of valuing shares do not. It rewards those companies that retain a high proportion of their profits for reinvestment in the business, and it allows market-tested yields to be incorporated into the valuation, rather than a more random variable.

There are also drawbacks to this approach. It works well only with those companies that have relatively straightforward balance sheets and a steadily growing business. Asset-based investments, or income-orientated ones, do not fit well with this approach but can nonetheless be legitimate investment choices.

Magic Number

32

Volatility

The Definition

Volatility is a statistical measure of past fluctuations in the price of a share, a market index, or the value of any asset. It is generally taken to be a proxy for risk. The higher the volatility of an asset, the greater is the chance of losing money when trading it. Volatility fluctuates over time. It is also a key component of option prices.

The Formula and its Components

Volatility equates to the standard deviation of the price of the stock, index, or other asset. Standard deviation is a statistical term calculated as a by-product of regression analysis. The calculation can usually be performed using a share's price and the statistical functions available in Excel. A ready-made spreadsheet for calculating volatility is available at *www.magicnumbersbook.com.*

A quick way of estimating volatility is as follows:

$$\text{Volatility} = [(\text{Period high} - \text{Period low})/2] \times 100/\text{Current share price}$$

In other words, take half of the difference between the high and low for the period in question and express it as a percentage of the share price (or, strictly speaking, the average share price) over the same period.

Volatility can be calculated over any period of time. The time period used should correspond to the maximum time over which you are likely to hold the asset in question.

WHERE'S THE DATA?

Share price data – you can find share price information, including 52-week highS–lows, in the pages of a financial newspaper. Investment software packages usually contain a means of accessing daily share price data for individual shares and indices. Links to suitable software providers can be found at *www.magicnumbersbook.com.*

Price histories downloadable into Excel can be obtained free of charge for a wide range of securities and markets from *www.thomsonfin.com*. There are various other local providers. Because volatility is a key component of option prices, many options exchanges may supply volatility data for the shares and indices in which they have listed options.

CALCULATING IT – THE THEORY

Figure 32.1 shows the different numbers required and how to use them to estimate volatility.

Figure 32.1 Calculating the "Magic Number" for ... Share Price Volatility

Universal Widgets Inc. has share price information as follows:

In the six months to December 2000

Average share price was $20
High–low over the period was $27–17
Volatility can be estimated as 25%
(working) .... [(27 − 17)/2] × 100/20

In other words, the difference between the high and low (10) divided by 2 (= 5) as a percentage of the price

CALCULATING IT FOR
THE NIKKEI

Figure 32.2 shows how the highlighted numbers from the Nikkei's price history can be used to produce the "magic number".

Figure 32.2 Calculating Estimated Volatility for the Nikkei Index

Estimating volatility works like this ...

Over the course of 2000, the Nikkei index ranged from a high of **20,505** to a low of **13,375**. It closed on 22 December 2000 at **13,423**.

The calculation is as follows:

50% of the difference between high–low is	3,565
(working)	(7,130/2)
This figure as a percentage of the current value	
(that is, estimated volatility) is	26.55%
(working)	(3,565 × 100)/13,423

However ...

The chart below shows the line of best fit for the Nikkei over the same period and a line representing one standard deviation from the line. This suggests that volatility is actually much lower than the estimated figure suggests (approximately 820 points, or 6%)

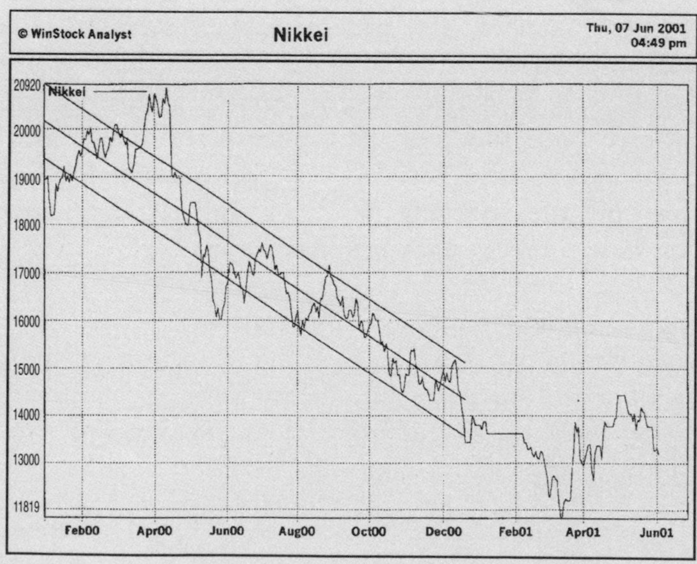

This is because the Nikkei has been in a steady downtrend for the year. The worth of the calculation can, however, be seen from the fact that – with only some rare exceptions – the price does not stray far from the limits of one standard deviation either side of the line

What it Means

Volatility should be intuitively easy to grasp. However, many investors find it confusing. Every investor knows that some shares move around more violently than others. Equally, there are times when an individual share goes through a quiet period. Little movement may occur in its price, and then it may inexplicably explode into life.

As explained earlier, volatility is normally expressed as a percentage band inside which the share price would be expected to remain for two-thirds of the time throughout a one-year period. A share with volatility of 20% standing at 100p would therefore expect to see its share price fluctuate between 80p and 120p – with only a one-in-three chance of it moving outside these bands.

The next step is to appreciate that the more volatile a particular share (other things being equal), the higher the risk in holding it. The reason is obvious: the greater the volatility, the more likely it is that a move will occur while you are holding the share that will result in your showing a loss.

The complication is that past share price performance may not be a reliable guide for the future. The statistical techniques described above measure the volatility based on the past performance of a particular share. This is known as historic volatility.

What any shareholder really wants to know is not what has happened in the past, but the expected future trend in volatility. Option pricing software allows for the calculation of volatility implied by the current market price of particular options. This can be useful, even if you only hold the underlying shares.

Links to providers of free options pricing software are available at *www.magicnumbersbook.com*, where there are also links to online calculators.

Volatility can change sharply over time for a variety of reasons, including market factors and events relating to the underlying shares. The volatility figure is also a key variable in calculating risk-adjusted returns, as expressed by the Sharpe ratio, which is the final "magic number" in the book.

Sharpe Ratio

The Definition

The Sharpe ratio (SR), devised by the American academic William Sharpe, is designed to calculate the true risk-adjusted return on an investment. It is calculated by subtracting the risk-free rate of return (see "Magic number" 27) from the annual total return on an investment. The result is then divided by the volatility of the investment in question (see "Magic number" 32) to arrive at the Sharpe ratio.

The Formula

SR = (Annualized return on the investment − Risk-free rate of return)/Volatility

The Components

The Sharpe ratio deals with the relationship between risk, return, and the risk-free rate of return. The idea is to separate out the extra (or "excess") return that derives from an investment over and above the risk-free rate, and then measure it against the risk involved. The risk in this case is defined as the volatility (or the standard deviation) of the return.

Annualized return – this is the percentage change in capital value in the course of the year (including any income received from dividends or interest), or if the return is on a monthly basis, the monthly return multiplied by 12.

Risk-free rate of return – since G7 governments are highly unlikely to default on their debt, there is virtually guaranteed repayment of capital – at the par value – on maturity. The yield to maturity on a G7 government bond is therefore an indicator of what the market views as the annual risk-free rate of return for that period of time.

Volatility – this is a statistical measure of past fluctuations in the price of a share, market index, or other asset. It is also generally taken to be a proxy for risk. The higher the volatility of an asset, the greater is the chance of losing money when trading it. Volatility equates to the standard deviation of the price of the stock, index, or other asset. Standard deviation is a statistical term calculated as a by-product of regression analysis. The calculation can usually be performed using a share's recent price history and the statistical functions available in Excel. ("Magic number" 32 has more information.)

Where's the Data?

Annualized return – this is the percentage price change over the course of the year, plus the dividend yield (if any) on a share or the "running yield" on a bond. It can be derived from information provided at financial or stock exchange web sites or from financial newspapers.

Risk-free rate of return – in this instance, this is the redemption yield on an appropriate government bond. This can usually be found from a financial newspaper or bond-related web site.

Volatility – this is calculated or estimated for the asset in question as described in "Magic number" 32.

Calculating it – the Theory

Figure 33.1 shows how two different investments can be compared using the Sharpe ratio.

Figure 33.1 Calculating the "Magic Number" for ... the Sharpe Ratio

Two separate investments have the following characteristics:

	Universal Widgets	**Allied Flanges**
Annualized return	10%	20%
Volatility	5%	25%
Risk-free rate of return is 5%		
Sharpe ratio is	**1.0**	**0.6**
(working)	(10 – 5)/5	(20 – 5)/25

In other words, although the apparent return on Universal Widgets is lower than that of Allied Flanges, the higher volatility of the latter means that its Sharpe ratio (risk-adjusted return) is lower. Universal Widgets is therefore the more rational investment to make

CALCULATING IT FOR

HEDGE FUNDS

Figure 33.2 shows how different hedge fund categories compare in terms of the Sharpe ratio. The figures are extracted from data at the web site *www.hedgeindex.com*, a joint venture between TASS-Tremont (a hedge fund performance database) and the investment bank Credit Suisse First Boston.

Figure 33.2 Comparing Sharpe Ratios for Hedge Fund Styles

The statistics relating to the performance of different hedge fund categories is shown below (figures taken are illustrative only and sourced from Credit Suisse First Boston Tremont Index LLC – *www.hedgeindex.com*)

Index name	Rate of return	Standard deviation	Semi-deviation	Sharpe ratio
CSFB Tremont Hedge Fund index	15.00	13.25	5.31	**0.69**
Convertible arbitrage	25.46	3.97	5.12	**4.93**
Dedicated short bias	0.24	26.27	24.34	**−0.21**
Emerging markets	15.04	23.19	15.06	**0.4**
Equity market neutral	15.06	2.19	3.33	**4.19**
Event driven	11.36	4.17	2.51	**1.31**
Fixed income arbitrage	7.2	1.19	1.42	**1.11**
Global macro	19.46	12.96	7.76	**1.05**
Long/short equity	19.07	22.23	11.21	**0.59**
Managed futures	−1.38	8.98	6.95	**−0.81**

Figures are for the 12 months to November 2000

The figure shows the wide variations in returns and risks, and how the Sharpe ratio reduces them to a common basis. For instance, the return from the "equity market neutral" category (15%) is nominally much lower than the convertible arbitrage category. After taking into account higher volatility, however, their respective Sharpe ratios are almost identical (over 4:1 in both cases). Returns by "equity market neutral" funds are achieved with lower risk.

What it Means

The Sharpe ratio is an elegant concept that can be applied to almost any investment that produces a return and where volatility can be calculated. It is most often used as one of the measures by which hedge funds are evaluated, but it can equally be applied to shares and to stock market indices.

There are other ratios that are derivations of the Sharpe ratio.

One is the Sortino ratio. The idea behind this is that what worries investors is not deviation in both directions around the mean return – as measured by standard deviation (or its synonym of volatility) – but only the deviation *below* the mean. Hence, the Sortino ratio is calculated in the same way as the Sharpe ratio: the numerator is the customary return minus the risk-free rate of return.

The only difference is that the deviation below the mean (known as the semi-deviation) or below some arbitrary target return is used as the denominator.

Appendix

Finding the Information

This appendix is designed to make it easy for you to find information to use and calculate "Magic numbers".

We concentrate on several areas:

- Financial portals for share prices and basic market data, including market capitalization, earnings per share, and dividend data.
- Ordering print-based material from companies.
- Official sources of information.
- Getting information from company investor relations web sites.
- Useful spreadsheets and calculators.

Links to all of the sites mentioned are also available at the *Magic Numbers* web site, *www.magicnumbersbook.com.*

Financial Portals

A portal is simply a gateway to the web – a site containing features and links relevant to your interests, a means of searching for information, and other facilities. Many have grown naturally out of so-called "search engines" such as *AltaVista* or Lycos, and some from newspapers. Some are pure start-ups.

However, if you are an active investor, there is a range of specialist financial portals you can use. Some are more relevant than others, but all share common themes.

Most financial portals allow you to access stock market prices on companies. They also feature financial news and bulletin boards, which enable you to interact online with other investors.

Financial portals usually give you access to share price charts and a facility whereby either one or more portfolios or "watch lists" can be monitored. Setting up a list of companies you are interested in and following them regularly is a good way of monitoring prices and news.

You may need to know the stock market symbols (sometimes called "ticker symbols") in order to set up a watch list. Sites differ in the ease with which data can be entered and changed. Some sites also allow watch list information to be viewed via a mobile device such as a WAP or 3G mobile phone or handheld PDA.

Individual company information (including accounts data) is usually also available at financial portals. Sites often link to other financial information and bulletin board comments direct from the quote page.

The following are a few examples of sites that contain comprehensive company or market information that you may find useful.

Bloomberg (*www.bloomberg.com*) has become known for localizing its popular broadcast content for individual markets, and the same is true of its web presence. Design and site layout varies little from market to market, and local languages are frequently used. English-speaking sites can be accessed from *www.bloomberg.co.uk* and *www.bloomberg.com/asia/*.

GlobalNet Financial, a financial information organization based in Los Angeles, has a range of sites covering individual local markets including the US, UK, the Netherlands, France, Sweden, Singapore, Hong Kong, and many others. Most sites are in local languages and all of the sites can be accessed from each other. Try *www.uk-invest.com* as the starting point.

The content is aimed at the private investor. There is a streaming share price ticker, commentary from leading pundits, portfolios, stock screens, bulletin boards, a very sophisticated Java-based charting tool, and other resources.

Several sites can be used to access information on a range of markets from a single place. **MarketXS** (*www.marketxs.com*) offers detailed company data across a wide range of North American and European markets, although you do need to know local ticker symbols to access it properly.

Market Eye (*www.marketeye.com*) was recently absorbed into *www.thomsonfin.com*. It covers a wide range of markets and is exceptionally easy to use. New users need to register and you may have to pay to access some content.

Comdirect's "market focus" section is outstandingly good for snapshots of a wide range of international markets, indices, and their constituents. English speakers can access the site from *www.comdirect.co.uk*. It is not necessary to be a client of the broker to access the site. Markets covered include all of the main ones in Asia, Europe, and North America.

Interactive Investor International has a site, at *www.offshore.net*, specifically dedicated to the concerns of offshore residents and investors. It also has, in addition to the parent site at *www.iii.co.uk*, English language versions at *www.iii.com.hk* for Asia, and *www.iii.co.za* for South Africa.

FTMarketWatch (*www.ftmarketwatch.com*) has comprehensive information on all main global stock markets and the companies within them, including price data and company information, much of which can be used to calculate "magic numbers".

Good UK-based sites include **ADVFN** (*www.advfn.com*). This has free real-time prices for UK stocks and the usual complement of portal accoutrements, including active bulletin boards. The company has a French language site (*www.advfn.fr*) and is also to launch in Japan.

Yahoo! Finance has a range of local language sites in various international markets with a broadly similar offering in each, focused around financial news and standardized company information. Start from *http://finance.yahoo.com*.

Those seeking Islamically sound finance or investments can check out **IslamIQ** (*www.islamIQ.com*), which also has companion sites covering stock investing and personal finance. This is a unique English language site aimed at Muslims. Conventional stock tickers are, for example, accompanied by automated indicators as to whether or not the company is regarded as sound from an Islamic standpoint. The sites also contain extensive news related to financial developments in the Islamic world.

Specifically Asian portals include: **Quamnet** (*www.quamnet.com*) which has real-time quotes, charts, news, and a daily market commentary. It also offers analysis and extensive news coverage in different industrial sectors, and has a page devoted to investor tools. Launched in 1998 in Hong Kong, the site also features a list of contributing columnists some of whom can be emailed with questions. **Stockhouse** (*www.stockhouse.com.hk*) has various sites including versions for Singapore (*www.stockhouse.sg*), Australia (*www.stockhouse.au*), and Japan (*www.japan.stockhouse.com*). The sites contain news, company profiles, brokerage reports, and interviews, although some content has to be paid for. Free membership includes bulletin boards, portfolio tracking, and email alerts on company and market news and portfolio updates.

Ordering Print-based Information

Companies are generally duty bound to send annual accounts to their shareholders, but will also often send them to other investors who may be interested. A telephone call to the company secretary or the investor relations department at the company, or even simply to their telephone receptionist, should allow you to order one easily.

Many company web sites now contain the email address of the company's investor relation officials. A spreadsheet containing a list of leading UK, European, and US companies that offer this facility is available at *www.magicnumbersbook.com*.

A simple email asking for an "investor pack", or a copy of the latest accounts, and giving your postal address, should suffice.

World Investor Link is an independent organization that operates in conjunction with leading business newspapers around the world to mail out copies of participating companies' annual reports free of any charge to anyone that requests them. You can find contact details for WIL in your local business newspaper or *The Financial Times* and *Wall Street Journal*. Reports can be ordered by telephone, fax, mail, or from WIL's web site at *www.wilink.com.*

Once your details are entered, provided you use the same computer, they need not be resubmitted each time you order a new set of accounts. Material is despatched (if in stock) within a couple of days. This is an excellent system, although as yet few Asian companies appear to be participating.

Information from Official Sites

Government company registration organizations, such as the Securities and Exchange Commission in the US and Britain's Companies House, are increasingly moving to collect and disseminate data electronically. The US is much further along this road than anyone else. The **EDGAR** (Electronic Data Gathering of Annual Returns) site is available at *www.sec.gov/edgarhp.htm,* although some unofficial EDGAR sites are easier to use. Try **10K Wizard** at *www.10kwizard.com* and **Edgar-Online** (*www.edgar-online.com*). A 10K report is a detailed annual report-style document that all US companies above a certain size have to file and make public. Similar quarterly reports are called 10Qs.

The UK's **Companies House** now allows online ordering of company accounts returns (covering two years) online at its website at *www.companieshouse.gov.uk* for £5 each payable by credit card. The documents can then be downloaded and printed.

Elsewhere, several stock exchange sites also contain links to the accounts data of listed companies. A list of the larger stock exchanges can be found at the "markets" page of the author's web site at *www.linksitemoney.com.*

Asian-orientated sites with detailed company information include:

AnnualReport.com.hk (*www.annualreport.com.hk*). This contains annual reports, latest company news and research, a market summary, free email alerts, and IPO news, all for Hong Kong-listed companies.

Finet (*www.finet.com.hk*). This is also a Hong Kong company database. It includes company profiles, business reviews and recent announcements, condensed annual report statements, and analyses.

Asiaweek (*www.cnn.com/ASIANOW/asiaweek*). This site has a list of the top 1,000 companies ranked by sales in million dollars. A detailed database of Asian companies is available for US$395.

Getting Information via Company Web Sites

Company sites have increasingly been used by more enlightened companies as a way of disseminating information to shareholders, the press, and other interested parties. Many sites contain a wide range of data, including annual reports available for downloading or viewing online, details of presentations made to analysts, news releases, share price information and price charts, and a range of other information.

Company web sites vary highly in quality. A summary of the data available for the companies used as examples in this book is given in the table on page 215. A list of company web site addresses for leading US, UK, and European companies can be found at *www.magicnumbersbook.com*. Links to these sites are also available at the author's web site at *www.linksitecorporate.com*.

Useful Spreadsheets and Calculators

A summary ratio analysis calculator can be found at the *Magic Numbers* web site (*www.magicnumbersbook.com*), as can the models for discounted cash flow analysis, reinvested return on equity, and volatility referred to in Part Five of this book. These spreadsheets require Excel 5 or higher.

These and a range of other spreadsheets and links to downloadable investment software covering charting, option pricing, personal financial management, and other topics can also be found on the "software" page at the author's website, *www.linksitemoney.com*.

Company	URL	Graphics	Annual reports available	Results info. available	Other press releases	Present-ations	"Live" share price	Share price chart	Investor relations email contact	Links	Country of origin
Ajinomoto	www.ajinomoto.com	Low	Yes	No	No	No	No	No	No	Yes	Japan
BP Amoco	www.bpamoco.com	Low	Yes	Yes	Yes	Yes	Yes	Yes	Yes	Yes	UK
Chugoku Electric Power	www.energia.co.jp	Low	Yes	No	Yes	No	No	No	No	No	Japan
DaimlerChrysler	www.daimler-benz.com	Low	Yes	Yes	Yes	Yes	Yes	Yes	Yes	Yes	Germany
Great Universal Stores	www.gusplc.co.uk	Low	Yes	Yes	Yes	No	Yes	No	No	Yes	UK
Hutchison Whampoa	www.hutchison-whampoa.com	Low	Yes	Yes	Yes	No	No	No	No	Yes	Hong Kong
Interactive Investor International	www.iii.co.uk	Low	Yes	Yes	Yes	Yes	Yes	Yes	Yes	Yes	UK
Kingfisher	www.kingfisher.co.uk	Low	Yes	Yes	Yes	Yes	Yes	Yes	Yes	Yes	UK
McDonald's	www.mcdonalds.com	Medium	Yes	Yes	Yes	Yes	Yes	Yes	Yes	Yes	US
NTT	www.ntt.co.jp	Low	Yes	Yes	Yes	Yes	Yes	Yes	Yes	Yes	Japan
RWE	www.rwe.com	Medium	Yes	Yes	Yes	Yes	Yes	Yes	Yes	Yes	Germany
San Miguel	www.sanmiguel.com.ph	Low	Yes	No	Yes	No	No	No	No	Yes	Philippines
Singapore Telecom	www.singtel.com	Low	Yes	Yes	Yes	No	No	No	Yes	Yes	Singapore
Solvay	www.solvay.com	Low	Yes	Yes	Yes	Yes	Yes	Yes	Yes	Yes	Belgium
Yahoo!	www.yahoo.com	Low	Yes	Yes	Yes	Yes	Yes	Yes	Yes	Yes	US

Index

F

G

H

I

K

L

M

N

O

P

Q

R

S

T

V

W

Y